Mexico Madness

ALSO BY EDUARDO GARCÍA AGUILAR

Essay

Celebraciones y otros fantasmas: una biografía intelectual de Álvaro Mutis

Delirio de San Cristóbal: Manifiesto para una generación desencantada

García Márquez: la tentación cinematográfica

Fiction

Bulevar de los héroes

(English translation: Boulevard of Heroes)

Cuaderno de sueños

Palpar la zona prohibida

Tequila Coccyx

Urbes Luminosas

El Viaje Triunfal

Poetry

Ciudades imaginarias

Llanto de la espada

Mexico Madness

Manifesto for a Disenchanted Generation

Eduardo García Aguilar

Translated from the Spanish by Jay Miskowiec

Aliform Publishing
Minneapolis

ALIFORM PUBLISHING
is part of The Aliform Group
117 Warwick Street SE
Minneapolis, Minnesota USA 55414
www.aliformgroup.com

Originally published in Spanish as
Delirio de San Cristóbal: Manifiesto para una generación desencantada
Mexico City: Editorial Praxis, 1998

First published in the United States of America by
Aliform Publishing, 2001

Library of Congress Control Number
2001132019

ISBN 0-9707652-0-7

Printed in the United States of America
Set in Garamond
Cover art and design by Edith García

Contents

A man sets out to draw the world. As the years go by, he peoples a space with images of provinces, kingdoms, mountains, bays, ships, islands, fishes, rooms, instruments, stars, horses, and individuals. And he discovers that the patient labyrinth of lines traces the lineaments of his own face.

Jorge Luis Borges, *Museum*

Preface

THIS ISN'T a book about Chiapas, that strange burst of flames which for months shook Mexico and prompted reflections in humanistic circles worldwide, at a time when one believed that rebellion against the absolute hegemony of vampire capitalism had been forever defeated and annihilated. The momentary media splendor of the Mexican Indians has already fallen out of fashion and barely remains fodder for newspapers or magazines. But if before that rebellion which began in January of 1994 any protest by those barefoot people was attributed to terrorism, madness, Marxism-Leninism, idiocy or a lack of common sense, now there is a slight crack of doubt about the absolute triumph of the all-powerful multinational financial dictators and their dogmatic final solutions. With that doubt in mind, those who don't worship the god of money, those who believe the inhuman greed of capitalism must be limited, still have a space to protest in that we must maintain, because the assent and order globalism wishes to impose has yet been completely achieved.

I know we don't have the right for our words to be heard in the highest spheres of power, because nowadays we suppose the wealthy and the stockbrokers possess the truth. But those rebels on the margins, as was in his time St. Francis of Assisi, do have a right to search for a people, a town, a city, a mountain where we might reflect upon our origins, the unending drama of our history, the culture we are forging, the past and future of the land of our birth and the world that contains it. The miracle of life is so attractive and its lights so bright, yet we move through it not knowing who we are, where we've come from or where we're going. The vast majority of human beings don't have the slightest idea what their existence, what their passage on earth means. In most cases their energy, tied to some inexplicable animism, is applied day after day to simply getting by or senselessly struggling for useless accomplishments like power, money, glory, force.

I made the following reflections in Chiapas, for I had always hoped to find a place where it was possible to stop a moment and consider the destiny of humanity, to look it head on in one of its strongest and most moving contradictions: that of the "ignorant, disposable" Indians confronted by the mechanism of power and gold.

Places for subtle reflection are usually quite strange — desolate cities in far-off countries, lost ports on some sea, ardent villages by overflowing rivers. In this case it was San Cristóbal de las Casas that took control of me, the Royal City as it was called centuries ago, with its pre-Hispanic colonial baggage and the contemporary bustle of those hurried men and emblematic figures: the bishop, the president, the guerrilla hero, the governor, the rancher, the soldier, the barefoot Indian, the tourist, the politician, the seminarian, the solemn white man. This is nothing compared with the great adventure begun 500 years ago, when indigenous people immersed in their own peculiar myths confronted a dream of giant ships on the ocean from which emerged bearded men dressed in strange clothing, sitting upon enormous unknown beasts that snorted with force. The foreigners in turn were astounded by those beings painted black and white adorned with feathers who emerged from the jungle or descended pyramids smelling of fresh sacrificial blood, shouting war chants against the invader and ready to cut out their beating hearts.

Here in this land that in colonial times was part of the Captaincy of Guatemala and later became part of Mexico, I lived another episode of that universal political fiction experienced by Sancho Panza on the Isle of Barataria. What's happening here is another chapter from the Latin American novel, and like all fiction when it's over it will survive only in photographs, songs or a hundred desolate tombs. And so I needed that cold highland city to journey within myself and this current period of Latin America, before and after the Cold War, and reconsider my years in Colombia, France, the United States and Mexico, a country burnished with a living Castilian and Indo-European syncretisms.

That journey includes the certitude that at this turn of the millenium, at a global level we are treading on the edge of a new cultural, economic, technological and political tectonic plate and therefore it is necessary to reconsider the crossways of the Americas, far from the naïve integrationist nationalism that has produced and still does produce so many evils and so much bloodshed; that is, to understand critically our congenital ills and lucidly re-establish the relation with our varied ethnic pasts and the "foreignness" we are part of by blood, taking in the diversity of Europe, especially Mother Spain, and the United States, the all-powerful neighbor we have more in common with than supposed. It's also necessary to deconstruct the dream of the noble savage and the good Indian — and let's especially be clear that the pre-Hispanic world wasn't some Eden, nor is there any possibility of returning to some mythic past, much less imposing it upon the majority of a country — as well as the guerillas and revolutionaries whose society would be naturally perfect and just, with neither vice nor totalitarianism. In the same way we are obliged to revise the conception of a pure, martyred Latin America whose poverty is caused exclusively by the evil gringos. We Latin Americans must first learn to be self-critical if we desire to escape the folkloric image that we refuse to let go of, tied as we are to a self-complacent delirium.

A reflection on the great chaos of Latin America must not be the sadomasochistic penitence it has been up to now. For such an enterprise, Mexico is a key country of analysis due to its simultaneous traumatic relation with the wicked Spanish stepmother and the ineffable Europe incarnated by the French invasion, and with the United States, insatiable devourer of its territory and culture. Mexico has at times resuscitated in foreign visitors passions of love and hate and its millenary character renders it ungraspable even to the natives: everything here is a sphinx, oracle, askew perspective; a mask, labyrinth, megalith. When you think you have found the answer, the question dissolves or becomes even more complicated. When the expert on Indians or the *Criollo* or some Icelander imagines he's on the verge of discovery, a great peal of laughter rings out. But in accord with its complexity, the country has also prompted throughout the centuries a wonderful permanent self-reflection among its poets, philosophers, historians, anthropologists and chroniclers. The development of Mexican thought offers an exemplary illustration for an investigation into the development of the Americas over time, from the Río Bravo to Patagonia.

And so in the streets of San Cristóbal de las Casas and the unfathomable countryside of Chiapas full of journalists, tourists on safari and photographers, I enjoyed the carnival of this new episode of Latin American "magic realism" and was tempted to reflect on what is happening to us at this late stage of history. At times some location overwhelms us at a precise moment and makes us question the oracle, "the formula of virtue or vice," as the Colombian poet León de Greiff once said, that rules over our lives. On one hand it's fascinating the technological development that presents us now with changes not long ago unfathomable, as intense as those of the nineteenth century, when artistic and social movements appeared that warned of the dark side of blind progress; aesthetic end-of-the-century literature and the social utopias of the commune and anarchism are such examples. The horrible world wars proved them right, showing technology unfurled in service of the annihilation of man. But on the contrary, during the last years of the twentieth century numerous peaceful protest movements have fortunately emerged whose goal is to stem the self-destructive aspects of blind planetary progress and so-called liberal ideology, intolerant of those on the periphery. Although cynical sectors of the intelligentsia are today as yesterday insensible to the sinister variants of progress, more and more humanist forces appear to confront valiantly the technocratic dogma that places cost/benefit analysis above all else.

In no way is this book about Mexico, much less Chiapas and the Zapatistas, a theme for which there are brilliant scholarly specialists. This is only the omnivorous delirium of a special correspondent and reader of Rubén Darío: an end-of-the millenium autobiographical inquiry into the past, the present and the very future of his continent, the Americas.

These are only life words, planet words, wind words, mask words.

Mexico City, July 1998

Preface to the English Translation

IT SEEMS A miracle that humanity survived the twentieth century and the planet has reached, beat up but still alive, the mythic year 2001, that magic date we first became aware of in the film *2001: A Space Odyssey*. Two world wars, as well as hundreds and thousands of economic, religious, ideological and ethnic conflicts sowed their devastation throughout the century at the same time the silent war of hunger and racism was waged. The delirious ideologies of Nazism, Maoism, and Marxism-Leninism, the dictatorial theocracies of the Middle East, and the destructive enterprise of all-powerful and impune vampire capitalism, each administered their dose of destruction to the planet.

In those distant years of the 1960s and '70s, in the middle of the Cold War and the most fantastic arms race in history, many people thought the earth would be destroyed by the explosion of thousands of nuclear warheads constructed at an astronomical cost by the two superpowers. The Gulf War in the early '90s, the first conflagration seen live and direct on television by millions of people in every corner of the world, showed us repeatedly the horrors of war: sirens wailing, bomb shelters with crying children, threats of chemical and biological war by a fanatical dictator, captured soldiers begging for their lives, clouds of acrid smoke covering the sky.

The fall of the Berlin Wall in 1989 had a double significance: it manifested the rebellion against the horror of Stalinist communism, but at the same time it gave to the ideology of barbarous capitalism the illusion that humanist rebellion had been categorically defeated, that history had come to an end, and that from then on we would be governed by the utilitarianism of neo-liberal gurus, that is, by a renovated version of the system described by George Orwell in his novel *1984* or seen in that premonitory film *Blade Runner.*

The civilized world had the fortune of defeating the totalitarianisms of first fascism and then Stalinism in the last century, but we have yet to defeat the blind and brutal forces of multinational capitalism, which if not controlled will lead us to a new totalitarianism of profit and wealth. The persistence of its unjust enterprise throughout the world has created at once a series of bloody movements of armed rebellion that end up becoming sources of sorrow and death in poor countries. The savage thirst for profit in this new technological era generates a savage thirst for vengeance in the hungry and impoverished throughout the entire world: two sides of the same dangerous coin. Stockbrokers and Third World guerillas both silence the opposition, both destroy the environment, both reap terror, both are corrupted and both must be stemmed by those everywhere who still believe in hope.

Nevertheless it's not crazy to say we have reason to be optimistic: despite the cases of genocide, hunger, and ideological and religious indoctrination, we reached the year 2001 alive. And moreover great sectors of the world's population, as much in the richest nations as the poorest, are beginning to join together in a multinational and multiethnic struggle against the abuses of uncontrollable grand capital and the tyrannies on the right and left that violate human rights and hold hostage millions on this planet.

Because the earth wasn't destroyed by the insane assassins of the twentieth century, we have a place to begin peacefully confronting those enemies of humanity, whether in the brokerage houses of London, Tokyo, Singapore and New York or in the lairs of fear in the jungles of Latin America, Africa, the Middle East, and Asia.

We must begin with the understanding that economic globalization and technological development are irreversible facts, products of the twentieth century, and that their forces can be channeled. We have to take advantage of them to reduce poverty, limit the ecological destruction of the planet, and open spaces of critical and intellectual freedom. As well we should use globalization to leave behind those fanatical nationalistic ideologies that discriminate on the basis of race, religion or class.

As a Colombian — child of one of the most violent countries on earth, a death machine where thousands of people are shot down every year and thousands more displaced from their homes at the violent hands of the ultra-right and the ultra-left financed by drug traffickers, industrialists and landowners — the unique and mediatic Zapatista uprising made me reconsider our continent and my own past.

The Zapatista rebellion has never had the goal of taking power but rather altering its course. And indeed many things have since changed in Mexico, chief among them that the longest ruling party on earth, the PRI, finally fell. In other parts of the world young people, fed up with the ridiculous reign of the yuppies and their adoration of the sacrosanct stock market, began reconnecting with the humanitarian dream of the defeated hippies from the '60s. In

Seattle during the meetings of the World Trade Organization, those youth were protesting against a world government based on money, just as in Tiananmen Square they had struggled against the tyranny of a communist dictatorship. In Europe they confronted the poisonous effects on the environment and food supply caused by a marketplace without rules and in Colombia they demonstrated for peace against the violence committed on all sides.

When I wrote *Mexico Madness: Manifesto for a Disenchanted Generation*, based on those events in Chiapas, Mexico, I wanted to reflect on the opportunity that we still have to confront the cold and calculating "free market." The rebellion of that band of Mexican Indians who refused to be humiliated any more after five centuries of savage domination seemed to me a symbol of a civil insurgency for this planet. The weakest, the most discounted, the "disposable," forced the most powerful to stop their triumphal celebration.

And so this book is a manifesto for our generation against despair: a reflection on our epoch, an accounting of our failures and a cry for peaceful struggle without ambition for power, so that the forces unchained by the marvelous technological and scientific development will be put to the benefit of humanity.

Paris, January 2001

Translator's note

EDUARDO GARCÍA AGUILAR describes himself as a professional foreigner. He has spent the last three decades living outside of his native Colombia, studying political economy and philosophy at the University of Paris before working as a journalist throughout the Americas. As a correspondent based in Mexico City for Agence France-Press, he covered topics from civil war in Central America to papal visits and economic trade conferences. At the same time he has had a prolific literary career, publishing a dozen novels, collections of short stories and poetry, and studies of world writers.

Mexico Madness: Manifesto for a Disenchanted Generation examines the phenomenon of a ragtag band of Indian rebels known as the Zapatistas, their charismatic leader Subcomandante Marcos, and the challenge they represent to the neo-liberal economic policies that Mexican administrations have blindly embraced in recent years. The Zapatista rebellion has never been about achieving power, but acknowledging the value of peoples who aren't tied to a cosmology of progress and success as defined by Wall Street or the World Bank.

The contemporary Mexican social and political situation provides García Aguilar a context in which to examine what it means to be Latin American in an era of a market-driven globalism dominated by the omniscient, omnipotent mass media. For someone who has spent over half his life as a journalist, he is most critical of his own profession, which he witnesses has turned human experience into a commodity to be bought and sold.

García Aguilar also looks at himself here: growing up in Colombia where he developed a love for his continent's literature, a kind of self-exile in Paris to escape the terror of his homeland, sojourns in San Francisco and New York, and finally almost twenty years in the biggest, greatest urb of the New World, Mexico City. The results are this "end-of-the millenium autobiographical inquiry into the past, the present and the very future of the Americas."

If this text is indeed a manifesto, then it proposes the most idealistic of agendas: that we esteem poetry and myth as much as political discourse and public relations, that we value mountains and village streets as much as automobiles and computers, that we listen to impoverished Indians and disenchanted youth as much as academics and stockbrokers.

And while *Mexico Madness* is based on a journalistic assignment García Aguilar undertook, he makes no pretense at being objective, dispassionate, "fair." This is a diary, and therefore it is straightforward and self-contradictory, lucid and enigmatic, reasoned and absurd, optimistic and desperate: truthful words and masked words.

Jay Miskowiec
Gringolandia, January 2001

On January 1, 1994, the nations of Mexico, Canada and the United States inaugurated the North American Free Trade Agreement (NAFTA), promising prosperity and progress to the entire continent. That same day, a group of Indian rebels in the southeastern Mexican state of Chiapas, whom the world would come to know as the Zapatistas, decided to crash the party.

One year later...

Monday, December 19

AT NOON we take off like a shot for Benito Juárez Airport in Mexico City because the Zapatistas have suddenly resurfaced in dozens of towns and villages. This morning a shopkeeper from Simojovel phoned to tell us about the arrival of masked soldiers to her town, and her trembling voice described in detail how they had posted guards on the street corners, entered stores and ransacked the mayor's office, and with a certain drama she related how they were just about to overrun her business. "It's the devil incarnate!" she exclaimed. Suddenly voices could be heard and the line was cut. It was necessary to go to Chiapas and feed the infernal machine of journalism — hydra of a thousand heads and furious forked tongues — with episodes from that enticing show about a rebellion at once pre-Hispanic and cybernetic, where a shot hadn't been heard for eleven months.

In two hours, after a comfortable flight to the regional capital of Tuxtla Gutiérrez, we're already flying down the excellent new highway to San Cristóbal de las Casas and the wind and cold fog immediately seduce me, taking me back to my childhood in Manizales, a city located near the Del Ruiz Volcano in the Andean *cordillera* of Colombia. A delicious cold wind stirs beneath the strange slanting luminosity of a blue sky that by the end of the afternoon creeps along in a dance of unreal designs, masses from a hyperrealist canvas in strange colors — magenta, purple, blood red, ruby, orange, steel gray — brushed on with a unique and palpitating millenary brilliance. An apt environment for pre-Hispanic gods or colonial monks standing before golden Baroque altars, walking through vast damp porticos beneath tile roofs that resound with the afternoon rain.

The pure air is delicious to breathe, so different here from Mexico City, that monstrous urb of twenty million inhabitants and thousands of avenues constructed for the satanic priests of the automobile god, destroyer of palm trees, parks full of elms, gardens, old mansions and historic buildings just to make way for another five million deified cars. This air doesn't seem real compared to the grayish magma that reigns over the metropolis, a mixture of dust and fecal matter combined with choking toxic gases; an unknown silence compared to the infernal noise, the congested streets, the bodies of children and old people trampled day after day, another statistic from that paradise of progress where the population takes pride in the city and celebrates the indiscriminate destruction of nature, where it celebrates strangulation, chaos, living death. San Cristóbal de las Casas is something else: situated, like the city of my birth, more than a mile above sea level and surrounded by coffee plantations, it envelops me with its human air and strange familiarity, its houses with terra cotta tile roofs, its encircling green mountains and welcoming breeze.

Colonial San Cristóbal was designed almost five centuries ago by its Spanish founder, Diego de Mazariegos — whose statue was toppled in 1992 by several Indians protesting the Quincentennial of the Discovery — for here the conquistadors found a climate similar to that of their own lands, far from the bats, predators and tropical heat;

the priests must have discovered an atmosphere conducive to old Spanish monasteries. Much later, in 1938, the Catholic English writer Graham Greene, author of *The Power and the Glory,* passed through the mountains of Chiapas on his way to this city, traumatized by the religious persecution in the neighboring state of Tabasco and hoping to find a mystical refuge from the country's chaos and the anticlerical Jacobinism he had witnessed in Villahermosa. But after the expropriation of the oil industry that damaged British interests and ruptured relations between the two countries, nationalist stirrings heated up in San Cristóbal. As the only Englishman in the city, Greene was flogged like a sacrificial lamb and recounted that he couldn't sit in the town square more than a few minutes before some passerby jeered at him. A victim of cutting remarks, humiliation and dysentery, Greene never forgave Mexico.

Nowadays you can get to San Cristóbal de las Casas from any place on the planet in less than twenty-four hours, but Fray Bartolomé de las Casas, bishop of what was then called Chiapa, who in the *Laws of the Indies* promulgated by Carlos V in 1542 had already decreed lessening the exploitation of the indigenous people, needed 424 days to reach this locality along with his contingency of Dominican brothers. The voyage, initiated in Salamanca January 12, 1544, and concluded in Ciudad Real March 12, 1545, was related in detail by Fray Tomás de la Torre in his diaries, a fragment of which is included in the appendix of *Travelers of the Indies*, by the Mexican writer José Luis Martínez. Forty-seven Dominicans and twenty-seven laymen left Spain, but due to shipwrecks and illness caused by the filthy conditions on board, they reached their destiny fairly reduced in number. We're only three months away from the 450th anniversary of that arrival which was so key to the spiritual make-up of this city in the cold lands.

The Argentine photographer Omar Torres and I settle into the house the press agency has rented for us on Francisco Villa Street, almost on the outskirts of the city, in a neighborhood where the only thing you hear at night are vehicles passing on the Pan American Highway on the way to Tuxtla or in the morning the lowing of some cow in the chilly nearby pastures. Omar sets up the transmitters, installs the darkroom for his film and unpacks his huge suitcase while I hook up the little Tandy computer, check some telephone numbers and place on the table a few books I've brought along: the 1947 second edition of D.H. Lawrence's *The Plumed Serpent* published by Editorial Losada, Malcolm Lowry's *Under the Volcano,* José Luis Martínez's *Hernán Cortés,* and Octavio Paz's *Labyrinth of Solitude.* I've got a little room with a view of the countryside, a telephone and an electric heater. It's a small typical middle-class two-story house with wooden floors, a big kitchen and a small outer garden.

We head over to the corner of Diagonal Centenario and Diego de Mazariegos on the way to the Zócalo, the main plaza, and a few blocks ahead we come to the Hotel Casa Vieja on María Adelina Flores Street, a colonial-style place with big wide beams that has become the den of journalists who enter and leave amidst useless gossip about a bulletless war, convinced they're in Sarajevo. I leave and go out walking down that street of low houses with terra cotta tile roofs, among which stands out the Hotel Diego de Mazariegos, the initial center of the journalistic wave. I want to be near the Cathedral in this cold weather and submerge myself in the city's back streets.

While I wander down these unknown streets, I recall the first days of the insurrection in 1994, which we had spent at our offices on the twenty-eighth floor of the Latin American Tower in Mexico City, spaced out by sleepless days and weeks of tension, filing stories about an event that was transforming the panorama of a country that had waited a long time for something to shake it out of its complacency. If things were surprising here in San Cristóbal, there were strange electric moments in the capital, rumors, a terrorist bombing (something that hadn't happened before), communiqués, fear among the populace and those gathered at the Café La Habana on Bucareli Street, near the Ministry of the Interior and the offices of the major newspapers where a lot of people thought things were finally coming to an end. You could already discern the certainty that gangsters from the "perfect dictatorship" would start generating more news, which is exactly what happened, in effect, with political assassinations and intrigues, foreign pressures, demonstrations by the opposition, capital flight, dirty business deals, Capone-style vendettas between drug traffickers, disinformation, in the end all the activity of that incredible transient world of politics and power common not only to Mexico but every country on earth, illuminated by the sinister imprint of palace succubae and Rasputins of every stripe, ultimately what is only fiction and masks. In Mexico City the vision at that time was of a country on the edge of an abyss, destroying itself little by little: either it continued its bloody fratricidal clash, a world-wide scandal created out of the massacre of malnourished Indians, or opted for a negotiated settlement.

That historical fracture in a country that had proven its stability over six decades stirred my passion for history. To imagine the seditious movement of powerful groups ready to take advantage of the raging currents, the activities of foreign espionage in this city which has always been an epicenter for it, the acts of delinquency and drug trafficking taking place in the vacuum of power, the intrigues threatening a coup and the imaginable palace anguish all excited my novelistic imagination. I don't believe this country has ever been closer to the legendary Ten Tragic Days of 1913, when after the death of a democratic president and dissident general, the father of Don Alfonso Reyes, a mob terrorized the central Ciudadela (now a library) and the surrounding streets, episodes seen in yellowed photographs from the era of burned, smoldering corpses.

A few years ago, following like some detective the adventures of the Rocambolesque poet and Colombian journalist Porfirio Barba-Jacob from his arrival to Mexico in 1907 to his death there in 1942, I found myself devouring the modern history of this strange land: the fall of Porfirio Díaz, the brief democratic summer, Zapata and Pancho Villa, the flight of President Eulalio Gutiérrez, the Ten Tragic Days, the dictatorship of General Victoriano Huerta, the years of Venustiano Carranza, Álvaro Obregón and Plutarco Elías Calles, the madness of José Vasconcelos; the years when the PRI, the country's virtual sole political party up until the end of the twentieth century, was formed; the support of different sectors for voting rights and the support extended by Lázaro Cárdenas to exiles of different tendencies and nationalities fleeing from Spain and other European countries besieged by the Nazi plague and the terror of the Second World War; the capital with its art, nightlife and sexy divas like Tina Modotti and Nahui Ollin and transient celebrities like Leon Trotsky, André Breton, Antonin Artaud, Graham Greene, Malcolm Lowry, Diego Rivera and Frida Kahlo; the Red journals, the daily newspapers, some of which disappeared like *El Demócrata* and *El Imparcial*; the living language of the Mexico City streets: pre-Hispanic words mixing with archaic expressions from the Vice Royalty one finds in Cervantes or Quevado, and then the sudden stamped influence of the United States; districts like the Centro Histórico, the Condesa, the Roma, Santa María la Ribera, La Merced, Polanco, Tacubaya, Mixcoac, Tlalpan,

Coyoacán; a hundred neighborhoods, streets and bars all blending together in a cocktail of interminable mirrors and voices, an unforgettable dance of specters that now come back this San Cristóbal December.

In a place seen for the first time, I suddenly find myself immersed in the novel of an exotic country where I have let myself be trapped, like so many other foreigners, by its veils and mysteries, its history of inexhaustible magmas and millenary stones, its geographical strata and bottomless abysses, its unclassifiable colors and eccentric cuisine, its great writers and painters who have left behind unforgettable art. Aromas, pyramids, convents, churches, beaches, cities in the north and south, hot regions and cold, mountains, volcanoes, dead poets like Luis Cernuda, the past impressed upon the blind walls of fantastic old mansions like the House of the Witches on the Plaza Río de Janeiro where I lived for three years, rain, sun, all embedded in the armor of a professional foreigner.

My debut in San Cristóbal takes place tonight: I go to the Cathedral and there behind the altar is the ineluctable and good-humored Bishop Samuel Ruiz. He is now the distant successor of the indigenist prelate Fray Bartolomé de las Casas, famous as well for recommending the importation of black slaves to alleviate the burden on the Indians. Ruiz stands behind the altar in a black cassock, a miter, and other purple articles, ready to begin a "sustained fast" in demand of a truce between the Zapatista rebels and the army, which since Monday have both seemed tense and stirring into movement after eleven months of relative inactivity. Yesterday the forces of the already legendary Subcomandante Marcos — a young, elegant and resourceful writer — infiltrated into new population centers once again with their fragile rifles, millenary faces from some Mayan stele, and uniforms of khaki shirts, green pants, simple boots, red bandanas, black ski masks, toy flashlights and rustic olive green military caps: converted into chic, fashionable guerrillas, into real but unique tourist attractions.

The press returns just to be present, as they had all year, to satisfy the gullet of the mass media fascinated by this new unfamiliar version of the broken-down dreams of Latin American revolutionaries. The most lucid here know this is another episode in a war between communiqués from the jungle and movements by ostentatious military convoys. The risk of a new armed conflict is almost null, taking into account the national trauma suffered from the initial combat in January when the deaths numbered in the hundreds, among the innocent Zapatista Indians, children and rebels, something Mexicans hadn't seen since the famous 1968 massacre at Tlatelolco or recalled in their collective memory since the deadly decades following the Revolution. On one hand small masked Indians, almost teen-agers, and on the other military forces, now quite alert and prepared, but unable to fire: in the middle, a country dominated by a regime holding power for more then seven decades, renewing itself every six years in a cyclical ritual where the previous *tlatoani* is submerged in ridicule and the new god is deified as a giver of hope; a country boiling over, at once fervent for and fearful of change, at the same time nostalgic for freedom and tyranny, terrorized at the possibility of losing the collective tyrant who is as protective and severe as Porfirio Díaz was in his day.

For the present worldwide technocratic project, which becomes harsher every day, these indigenous people out of the past are "disposable." It's quite possible that in the next few centuries we'll approach that world visualized by Ridley Scott's *Blade Runner* and some contemporary apocalyptic writings: a rich elite of aparatchiks hidden in their bunkers and a huge anachronistic population of disposable poor people, more distanced than ever from technological advances, just dead weight, "useless" people like these Indians who don't fit into the society of progress. A miserable population that would be very comfortable in Jonathan Swift's satire of 1729, *A Modest Proposal,* which suggested converting the poor children of Ireland into a delicious meat "somewhat dear" and "proper for landlords," because "a young healthy Child well nursed is a year Old a most delicious nourishing and wholesome Food, whether Stewed, Roasted, Baked, or Boiled; and I make no doubt that it will equally serve in a Fricasie, or a Rougoust."

The conflict in Chiapas has become famous because, whether or not guided by young ideologues and white clergy, it is the last cry of the discarded before they disappear, as is already taking place in Africa, in the former Yugoslavia, in Chechnya, where blacks, Muslims and nationalists are massacred in an apocalypse that almost nobody cares about anymore. For the triumphant project of the great uncontrollable itinerant capital of the world, those rich lands full of innumerable wealth must be rid of these slovenly, obstinate people from the past who reproduce like rabbits, who don't eat hamburgers and who represent an increasing problem because they are so obsolete. Headed by some young idealist, those Indians think they are sensitizing their fellow citizens in the cities who by the millions, young and old, turn their back and leave them to the mercy of what are called here the "Sandalistas," the neo-hippie humanitarians of the world who are members of utopian civic associations, or journalists who will be called back by their bosses to the office and then condemned irremediably to oblivion, while the attractive massacres of thousands and thousands of "useless" blacks in Africa, "extremists" in North African or Arab countries, "fanatical and skeletal" Hindus or

Kurds or Gypsies on the edges of Europe and the former Soviet Union continue. The Creole high-level officials with a little bit of Aztec blood and the hundreds of thousands of comfortable urban *ladinos* favor the quick elimination of that shameful weight of those millenary races that prevent them from reaching the white Anglo-Saxon First World. The same thing happened in Brazil with the Amazonian Indians who opposed the destruction of their habitat, the lungs of the world, and with other monolingual aborigines of the continent not eliminated quickly enough by the Spanish or by that triumphant tacit philosophy of grandiose modern capital which has neither flag nor law and has already become the earth's most ominous alien.

For that reason Samuel, whose proclivity towards the Indians disturbs the Vatican, is here, silent before a smaller gathering of the faithful, fewer in number than the reporters, photographers and cameramen of every sort who look uncomfortable among the parishioners. He ends the homily, descends with a pachydermal slowness and to the sound of canticles passes down the center aisle of the church toward the chapel of La Inmaculada, accustomed already to the flash bulbs and kneeling photographers who have been following him and the smoke wafting from his censer. He has just begun another of his protagonistic acts from thirty-five years as bishop, hated by the rich and the conservative high prelates who censor him for his "doctrinal fault" of taking the side of the region's Indians — the Chamulas, Tzeltales, Tzotziles, Choles, Mames, Tojolabales, among others — he supports or "manipulates," according to the lens through which he's viewed. It has been a long time since I've seen a bishop up so close, that kind of specimen, supposedly asexual and good, which has exerted such great influence over the continent since the arrival of the Spaniards.

In Latin America, with a few honorable exceptions, Catholic bishops have been allied with the region's wealthy class, armies, political thieves and assassins. Fat, greasy, rich, gluttonous, racist, ass-lickers of the powerful, the bishops have solidified bigotry and humiliated the poor by taking the side of the ranchers and the military, of genocidal dictators and supposedly democratic presidents. My father, a good Jacobean liberal, hated them because in my country they were always on the side of the hegemony of the Conservative and Liberals, different sides of the same ignominious coin, who persecuted and killed those who disagreed with them. On one hand they talked of chastity and morality and on the other, in secret, they practiced *turbia delecti* abhorrent beyond words while remaining silent about the abuses committed by party bosses who took advantage of the weak and women. The complicity of the continent's Catholic hierarchy with the powerful in order to oppress the downtrodden is so odious that no doubt a primal anticlericalism is justified.

In 1989, during John Paul II's visit to Mexico I followed the pontiff to a number of cities including Mexico City, Veracruz, Aguascalientes, Durango, Monterrey, Tuxtla Gutiérrez, Zacatecas and Villahermosa, without missing one of his public acts, at times separated from him by just a few feet, like once in the church San Juan de los Lagos, another time perhaps ten feet away, sometimes standing at the front of a delirious crowd when he climbed imposing scenic stages surrounded by cardinals and their assistants, accompanied by the voices of sacred choirs or the sound of the multitude, like in Zacatecas or Durango, this last location beneath a stifling desert sun. I saw him walk, perform miracles, pray, climb stairs, tell jokes to young people, stir up the crowd, sing, deliver solemn speeches, ordain priests, marry people. Ten days, one after the other, in the fair of a delicious trip that went new places every day on a plane filled with journalists from all the over the world and people from the Vatican with whom we'd end the evening half-drunk listening to music in some bar.

But this time it is Bishop Ruiz three feet from me, standing before a writing desk, his gaze directed toward the Virgin flanked by enormous angels in this cold chapel, ice-cold one might say, where he has decided to fast until peace is reached. He is the archetypal seventy-year-old bishop — round, well-fed, rather short, his belly covered by a purple sash, wearing glasses, like an old village priest in some Balzac novel. Shortly before the rebellion he was almost defrocked by the Vatican, but he finally won that battle. *Tatik* the Indians call him and when he puts his hand on the black heads of those survivors of the conquest, one can understand the centenary force he possesses as heir of De las Casas and the first Dominican adventurers who arrived to the Valley of Jovel.

For a long time I have realized how marked I am by the Catholic cultural atmosphere I grew up in during the '50s, blended with my father's radical Jacobean atheism. Grandmothers, aunts, my mother, my mother's friends, schools, teachers, priests, governors and presidents, cardinals, popes, they all surrounded and nurtured us with those rites and ceremonies. The memory of nocturnal processions in my cold city near the volcanoes is indelible: people singing hymns while walking down the streets and avenues, carrying lighted candles and those impressive saints on placards such as the Virgin of Sorrows and the bloody Nazarenes, are forever ingrained upon our minds and remain part of our culture, neither Jewish nor Muslim nor Protestant nor Buddhist. To be here before this short astute Bishop Ruiz is in a way quite familiar to me. To see those blessed women from the region praying the rosary as did my Grandmother Mercedes and my aunts is as natural as the landscape of this coffee region of Mexico near Guatemala on this icy Monday evening.

Besides the ineffable affected piety of our grandmothers, I'm overwhelmed by the imagery of the altars, retables, church icons, the Baroque temples of New Spain that possess a millenary delirium, the interminable golden tapestry woven upon the cupolas. I can gaze for hours at the work of the New World artisans in modest village churches five centuries old where the crown decided to extend Christianity by blood and fire. I like knowing that the Indians molded the figures and collaborated in the construction of the churches; during festivals I love the movement of the villagers, the smell of the flowers, the cool atmosphere within the churches where the faithful come — thin, grimacing old women, men dressed in white, little boys with new haircuts, and inside those walls they live out their literature and their collective imagination, attracted by an ancestral force. Around the church transpires the life of our real people, that is, grandmothers, women, children, old people: the existence of the poor who have no way to transform themselves except by connecting with Biblical absurdities, at least when they aren't converted into Swift's fricassee or slaves of television.

For centuries religion has been the only refuge of the disposable and not even television, converted into an imaginary possible alternative with its plastic stars, has been able to displace it. In the already inevitable world dominated by technological aristocrats, it is possible that those religions, each with its own particular attributes, will soothe as always the muddy, dirty abandonment of thousands of millions of marginal human beings before economists find a quick and efficient way to eliminate them from this terrestrial hell and send them to their opiated heavens, that is when they're not turning them into sausages. Why did the madness of modernization over the last few decades make us lose perspective and distance ourselves so much from Latin American cultural reality, one definitely of villages and their churches, religious festivals that reconcile different traditions, fireworks, processions, tables piled with food and fresh juices, everything animated by a wonderful band playing off key? Every attempt to distance our people from religion has been and will be useless.

In Mexico the Spanish adopted their patriarchal religion to the matriarchal pre-Hispanic religion and used the indigenous totalitarianism for their own hegemony. During the twentieth century, with the Virgin of Guadalupe on one hand and the identification of the party of the state on the other, in Mexico was created the "perfect dictatorship," as termed by the Peruvian writer Mario Vargas Llosa, not by accident from a millenary country whose indigenous people lived through a collision with the Spaniards in many ways similar to Mexico's. Mexico and Peru were the first great Spanish vice-royalties and by means of a holocaust they imposed a new faith upon the powerful, constructing new empires and stone temples. Things have changed. There used to be some space for these people in the immense expanse of the continent: now they're no longer "viable," as they say in the new technocratic language, for the world that unfailingly awaits us. Poets, thinkers and Indians are now disposable, but it will be difficult to finish us off.

Each person lives their cultural origins as they can. Muslims, Hindus, Jews, Protestants, and animists have the right to drown in their madness or reject it. In our case this origin is definitely Catholic, with its cruelties and Baroque qualities, so it is worthwhile rescuing its impressive aesthetic traces, as long as one is attentive to the injustices of the clergy and its evil imbrication with terrestrial power, because the priests of reason and progress can be just as sinister as the Catholic priests. First there was the anti-Catholic crusade of the positivist Reform, then came the fashionable post-war ideologies and a lot of people thought they could barter their origins for a gelatinous liberal rationalism or a Marxist gospel in all its horrendous varieties, whether Chinese, Soviet, or Cuban. Now that all that has gone up in smoke, many people have been abandoned and will perhaps return to the Baroque Latin American religiosity, to a Byronic romanticism, to an end-of-the-century dandyism, to a Rousseauian environmentalism, to the revindication of their sexual differences. A few will turn again towards the attractive aesthetics of their original religion, others will head towards a neo-Nazi fanaticism whose shades within Latin America are as varied as the region of its origin.

Why don't we let ourselves be Baroque, romantic, environmentalist, as Europeans were in their time Goths who, encrusted in their Romanic past, dreamt of the flames and exotic airs of the distant Orient, who conducted the Inquisition, who were fanatics of Calvinist reform and who finally fell victim to the holocaust of their madness? Let's allow our imagination to flow in the Gothic fugues of the hot lands, as Álvaro Mutis would say of this marvelous tropical New World of slanting suns and exuberant vegetation, eternal crystal forms beneath cupolas through which filter the rays of the sun, the movement of dust, the cry of lepers.

We are the ancient ones, said the splendid blind old man Jorge Luis Borges. The delirium of progress is only a fragile and short episode in the life of man: we go farther into the past than we do into the future. We live on a new cultural and technological tectonic plate whose slippery movement is like some crazy iceberg in the Arctic. We are heading in an ineluctable way towards regions barely imagined, just like those who lived astonished on the verge of the Renaissance, and it seems ridiculous to cry at change, for it is firm and inevitable. But the power combined from churches and sole political parties from the past might not be ready to accept its own irremediable bankruptcy or avoid all totalitarian temptation.

In the last few decades man has achieved, thanks to his intelligence and effort, a series of undeniable advances, but at the same time other sectors of greedy and predatory humanity are leading the world toward ecological disaster using the arms of religion, the politics of technology markets, and Orwellian television. While the smallest part of humanity enjoys these advances, unthinkable barely a decade ago, the majority every day becomes further distanced from them by the vampires of progress. But it might be worth asking whether this relegated part of humanity truly needs and wants to join that world of terrible and forceful fantasy, even though we don't know where it leads us or whether this fictional world will go bankrupt after years of splendor as did Egypt, Greece, and Rome.

Tatik has begun his fast, wrapped up in a blanket to protect him from this intense December cold. The journalists have already left and he remains surrounded only by the blessed women in solidarity with him, among them a beautiful dark young woman in jeans, military boots, scarf and a fine leather jacket that looks like it used to belong to some London rock star. She gazes at the crowd with her somber black eyes.

Tuesday, December 20

IN THE MORNING we head towards Simojovel on narrow dirt roads out past San Andrés Larráinzar, hoping to find real live Zapatistas. The Argentine photographer Omar Torres drives the pick up and we are accompanied by his colleague Dan, a gringo from Los Angeles, California, a thirty-year-old ex-soldier and arms expert who describes to us in detail the characteristics of the vehicles and weapons we come across at the checkpoints. Dan looks a lot like the novelist Philip Glendenen I met in San Francisco in 1980: he's short and stocky, wears a baseball cap, talks little and has a good sense of humor. We've chosen the roughest road, for the other way, the final part of the route that starts in Puerto Caté, was blocked with enormous wide trenches dug by the rebels. After passing through the famous village of San Juan Chamula, full of strange capricious Indians who love alcohol, we arrive to tense and desolate San Andrés Larráinzar, also under the control of the Zapatistas, officially known as the Ejército Zapatista de Liberación Nacional (EZLN), the Zapatista Army of National Liberation. The plaza is missing the normal movement of such villages and just a few silent men gather on the street corners in small groups, looking indifferently at the intruders. I go into the church and there are dozens of Tzotzil Indians, mostly women, sitting next to a band of harps and other instruments that plays beneath an image of a saint surrounded by burning candles. They wear amazing hats with multicolored ribbons, cotton pants, sandals and ponchos with colored stripes and speak their language among themselves. I ask an Indian covered by a black wool cape who stands beside his wife, a beautiful woman with white, white teeth, how everything is going and he tells me he doesn't know anything and immediately turns around and heads toward a coop in the patio and its clucking chickens.

The church is decorated with innumerable branches of white and red flowers that impregnate the atmosphere with a funereal smell mixing with the incense. The slow, sad music of the harp and maracas begins to resound along with the strange lilting Tzotzil voices that seem almost Baroque. Outside the church on the street corners still stand those silent men with impenetrable eyes, beings from another planet, from another world, taught to keep their thoughts to themselves, to measure their words and carefully mete them out to strangers. There's no other way to live in the distrustful world of these lost regions where politicians occasionally come to make promises and then don't return, a place where their millenary stigma is a silent resistance to other tribes or the white Spanish invader or the abusive, plundering *mestizo*. The centuries haven't passed here. This is the reign of silence.

We say farewell to the men with frozen gazes, turning down their request for a ride; we drive through the town on a windswept, rising highway past desolate broken-down houses; suddenly a man on a tractor appears who asks us where we're going, and after questioning us a short while he lets us by. Villages where people dry their coffee unfold before us, sordid little plots of land and in one of them we're detained by a group of drunken men, Indians and poor mestizos with glassy eyes, who slur something at us in alcohol-laden breath and demand money to pass by. Farther on the highway leads to more beautiful places and a dreamy landscape opens before us: a great mountain extends up one flank of the horizon, rising high into the blue sky in an expanse of endless blue-green precipices, and on the other side are high rocky outcroppings and ridges of desolate green, covered by slowly moving cottony clouds. You imagine that during pre-Hispanic times some of their gods lived in such altitudes of unequaled beauty and suddenly you're confronted with the image of some man carrying a bundle of firewood in the trees or playing a flute, immersed in a world far from the madness of modernity. They look the same now as they always have and old women with long braided hair do their tasks in the smoke of wood fires while their daughters, dressed in blue skirts embroidered in red, play and run around the wire fences beside the burros, chickens and dogs. Thus time passes in the canyons and mountains.

The first Zapatistas appear, fifteen or so of different ages, dressed in their typical clothing, some armed with .22 caliber rifles and others with much more powerful AK-47s. They've blockaded the highway with tree trunks and stones and stop us for questioning. A short masked Indian with a rigorous gaze inspects us one by one, looks over the camera equipment, asks about our activities while others look on silently and still others stand with arms ready, just as they had appeared in thousands of photos throughout the year. He takes our press passes to his chief who suddenly returns to tell us we can't pass because our credentials don't say "war correspondent" as required by the Zapatista command. We are in the presence of a real army and not just some peasants blocking highways as they said in Mexico

City and if we knew the true extent of their control in the region we wouldn't believe it. The twenty-thousand journalists who have crossed through these lands throughout the year dream of such encounters in the perfect setting with flesh-and-blood Zapatistas. I have to confess it's the first time I've seen them "live" and it seems like passing an initiation after ruminating about their destiny for a year on the twenty-eighth floor of the Latin American Tower in Mexico City. Like an entomologist I look over head to toe these men standing there while Dan and Omar eat them up with their cameras. In any Latin American country situated beyond Suchiate guerillas have been part of the common landscape for decades, but the novelty is that we're here in Mexico, a country which until recently had appeared stable.

I'm named Carlos for an uncle who disappeared during the period of *la violencia* in Colombia, around 1953, and I was born one September 7th in a country where day after day hundreds of people died in the most atrocious way. The Gothic rabble came and burned villages, raped mothers and daughters in front of their men and then forced the violated women to witness the horrible torture of their grandfathers, husbands, uncles and fathers who had their tongues and genitals cut off, their eyes gouged out and then were macheted to death; they would rip open the stomachs of pregnant women and toss babies in the air, laughing while they caught them on the end of their machetes. The government of the Conservative Party decided to eliminate the Liberals, who were forced to hide in the mountains or flee to other cities, as described in *Viento Seco,* that terrifying novel by Daniel Caicedo, a young author from that period that my father used to read and once recommended to me so I would remember the horror of that nameless war which left hundreds of thousands dead and filled canyons and ravines with rotting corpses picked over by vultures.

They gave me the name Carlos for that guerrilla uncle who disappeared but whom I would later meet when he was already an old man, in Ibagué, surrounded by his children of all ages. That uncle showed me, on the moving day we met, photos of the legendary rebel chief Guadalupe Salcedo and his troops and documents from his youthful armed adventure, and then he took me hunting in the mountains to show me the agility and strength he still possessed. That night we ate *boruga,* armadillo, around a campfire as they used to do in the mountains, a meat that moreover brutally poisoned me and left me delirious and bedridden an entire day. Stories about ambushes, accounts of the sudden changes in fortune of the immortal Tirofijo, anecdotes of great bandits like Sangrenegra or Desquite who left in desolate ruins any place they passed through, fed the Colombians of my generation and those before us in a country whose violence has yet to cease.

Family legend mentions the first wife of my Uncle Carlos, a beautiful fair-skinned woman, the star of family photo albums, who perished beside the crib of her two children from a ricocheting bullet during a gun battle in a village near the Magdalena River. They used to tell us the bullet went around the village square several times, hit the church bell, killed a hummingbird and then entered the house, despite her having closed the windows and taken refuge in the nuptial bedroom; it still sought her out there to kill her, and then my uncle disappeared and became a family phantom remembered through my real name, Carlos Eduardo. A typical story of Colombians, improved upon, augmented, made Baroque by the ceaseless eloquence of grandparents, aunts and uncles, friends and acquaintances drunk on *aguardiente.* We grew up with those heroes right before us, and in addition to the terrible bandits who avenged the atrocities with yet more death could be added the guerrillas from the '60s: Che Guevara and Tania, the Cubans Fidel Castro and Camilo Cienfuegos, the Colombians Tulio Bayer, Camilo Torres, Fabio Vásquez, Rendón and so on until coming to the Tupamaros, the Montoneros, the Sandinistas and the Shining Path. In addition to the Catholic imagery we inherited from our grandmothers and aunts, we were left that group of revolutionary saints who confronted the governments of Latin America, something we cannot free ourselves from and which is an essential part of our identity.

Those Zapatista guerrillas in Chiapas are a kind of miraculous apparition: their original ski masks, their red bandanas, their brown shirts, their green pants, their fragile boots, their stick rifles seemed to me truly unheard of for a country like Mexico that had managed to live in relative stability for most of the century, thanks to the submission of its desperate people and the terrible arbitrariness of its political system, a regime whose crimes have always remained hidden thanks to the nonexistence of an autonomous judicial system and the corruption that reigns under the mafioso law of *omertá*. These diminutive men, with their millenary eyes and inconfutable skin, had the valor and courage to demonstrate once more that in Latin America episodes of rebellion will remain common currency despite the dreams of the technocratic class, who are determined to be like those from the North, so well analyzed by Max Weber in his book, *The Protestant Work Ethic and the Spirit of Capitalism,* who possess a kind of sterile ethics that might be respectable and valid for other cultural environments but not for ours, a mixed Hispano-Arabic Catholic Baroque hedonist chaotic race that is by no means Puritan.

January 1, 1994 — the very day Mexico, considered until then the teacher's pet of neoliberalism, was about to enter the North American Free Trade Agreement (NAFTA) with the United States and Canada, an accord which according to elegant government officials would deliver wealth and carry the country and continent along the path toward First World prosperity, spattered with arrogant yuppies with houses in Houston or Miami and submissive laborers — that same happy day a few Indians broke upon the world like bulls in a china shop. The impact of their gesture was even more impressive because it was believed, by naïve minds, that the age of guerrilla activity in Latin America had been abandoned. In a letter to Marcos, the Mexican writer Carlos Fuentes remarked that only a few years before "you would have been marked with the branding iron of anti-communism. You are the first post-communist actors in the Third World. Your aspirations can no longer be occulted or perverted as a world-wide Soviet conspiracy. Only those shipwrecked in the Cold War, those left without maniacal enemies, could believe that. Now we must confront social problems without ideological excuses." The certainty among the happy canticles of businessmen and the wealthy in general that the marginalized were defeated and revolutions had ended didn't last very long.

It only takes a bit of common sense or historical perspective to realize that social tensions between the powerful and the dispossessed continue to exist and the episode of communist ideology was only an accident in a centuries-old dance of tyrannies and rebellions that in the future will discover other discourses and other saintly figures. I want to insist on that. I was referring to my uncle the guerrilla, who would now be over eighty, because at the turn of the new millenium the cycles of history repeat themselves: in Colombia a large part of the country is dominated by different factions of guerrillas that the government can do nothing about. The same thing happened a century ago during the legendary War of a Thousand Days, fodder for our grandparents' imagination. Today things are relatively calm in the Americas, but it won't be long before things erupt again. In Venezuela Captain Chávez is a hero, in Peru the war is concealed and contained, and in the rest of the continent, to the extent that the situation is getting worse for everyone, the caldron is simmering and the pot is about to boil over.

Latin America feeds upon its heroes and saints because the cyclical episodes and cultural mix so demand it: at this new millenium the situation is as fragile as it was during the nineteenth century, today's operatic democracies caricatures of tyrannies from another time. Works like those by Romulo Gallegos, José Eustasio Rivera, Jorge Icaza, José María Arguedas, Martín Luis Guzmán, and Miguel Ángel Asturias are as relevant now as when they emerged: the Amazon rubber-tappers, the barbarous ranchers in the Venezuelan plains, the closed white racist aristocracy of Guatemala, the military assassins in South America who still survive, the mere reflection of modernity, could make one believe in the decades of the '80s and '90s that the Protestant ethic, with its sterile and well-ordered McDonald's and Kentucky Fried Chicken, had definitively conquered the Indian, African, Arab and Spanish Latin America. Everyone sang the end of Revolution, the beginning of an era of honest and incorruptible businessmen respected by their thankful employees, but the Zapatistas threw the awkward reality right in their face. This is neither for the good nor the bad, it's just the way it is. I don't believe in a radiant future nor in red and black paradises to come.

We all know that guerrillas who take power often turn immediately into phalanxes of new and odious rich people. On the contrary, future centuries, in the measure that the population grows and nature is destroyed by progress, are threatened by an apocalypse of plagues and godless, lawless wars. History is viewed by theoreticians as if it were ordered, but it's as unpredictable and undulating as a typhoon in the middle of the ocean. Here is the evidence of this compressed wheel of fortune, of history going nowhere. The twentieth century began with the Bolsheviks and ended with parades honoring the Czar's family through the streets of St. Petersburg and Moscow. Thousands gave their lives in Spain fighting the monarchy and now the king is adored by the masses. The bloodsucking communist regimes of Eastern Europe fell and all the old nationalisms were given free rein with their cohorts of death and hunger and suddenly African dictators like Idi Amin Dada, Mobutu and Bokassa look like little altar boys next to the assassins from the end of the century.

Finally the Zapatistas detaining us bar our entry into their territories and order we go back. A helicopter coming from the other side of the mountain flies overhead, turns and seems like it's coming at us. The Zapatistas are frightened and take guard. A few disappear into the brush, agile as lizards, others take up positions with their arms in ravines or behind stumps. Farther ahead others fell more tree trunks and put more rocks on the highway. For a moment the helicopter really does appear like it's heading right at us, but it finally banks and is lost behind the mountain. "Get out of here, get out of here," the Zapatistas tell us, not without first letting themselves be photographed.

A hundred meters farther on the commander, covered by his ski mask, pedals his bicycle and escorts us toward a settlement with an antenna, electric cables, activity, playing children. Nobody changes their clothing, everywhere are bases of support, everyone is out of Lope de Vega's *Fuenteovejuna*. It's impossible to do away with the Zapatistas because they'd have to napalm these lands into oblivion. The population's complicity with the Zapatistas is obvious, despite the banners and official slogans plastered onto the walls. On a street corner a Tzotzil family laughs and celebrates around an enormous six-foot snake they've just killed. Next to the highway are still those impassible men with impenetrable gazes. An Indian girl named María smiles at us, too beautiful to be devoured by the period of her history here and turned into that skinny grim-faced old woman with gray braids and dirty hair, bare feet and flaccid breasts who laughs and laughs next to the dead serpent. The eternal serpent that returns. The serpent of a history out of time.

When we get back to San Cristóbal we have to plan another route for the trip to Simojovel, for they say the army is already moving rapidly to "reconquer" the area. We lunch in a place run by a crazy old man who enjoys joking with the tourists and journalists. The hot tortillas are steaming, the aroma of *mole* and good coffee wafts in the air. On the highway to Tuxtla, before the turn off to La Tijera, are various checkpoints and the military brandishes its presence knowing they can't use it against the "faceless men," the original ones who Hernán Cortés, Pedro de Alvarado and Diego de Mazariegos saw four-hundred and seventy years ago. The soldiers are all very healthy and well fed, quite a few are Indians and others are mestizos, in nice uniforms and shiny helmets. They smile beside their armored jeeps, tanks and trucks. When we get to Puerto Caté they don't even check us at the guard post. The soldiers and officers joke around next to even more powerful vehicles. The highway is empty to Simojovel and just as happened to us in the morning with the Zapatistas, at five in the afternoon we see a sudden new apparition: an impressive green convoy slowly heads to "retake" the town.

Retake is one way to put it, because yesterday, Monday, a few dozen diminutive Zapatistas stormed into the central plaza, requisitioned a few merchants, lifted their rifles and it also seems some money, and left "in terror" the area's storekeepers and wealthy who locked themselves in their homes, from where they called the state capital of Tuxtla requesting military forces be sent. Here come the soldiers down the highway, filling one ditch after another: some ten trucks replete with Public Security, Military Police, soldiers, and bringing up the rear are tanks, armored vehicles and jeeps with tinted windows, like in some movie with Jack Palance and Lee Marvin. Mr. Stuart, a US diplomat, the typical soldier — six-feet-four, fat and white with sporty affectations, among them the infallible baseball hat — supervises their movement and salutes the captains. One of them takes leave with a friendly, "OK, Mr. Stuart," when I approach and try to ask some questions. "Why did you let those photographers through?" asks Stuart. "With their credentials they can pass, but if you want I can make them go back," obediently responds the Mexican officer.

It's getting dark and we've been stopped here a long time next to the twisting highway. What should usually take no more than an hour and a half, because of the convoy, the first of its magnitude in eleven months, has taken more than five hours. A lot of journalists have already gone back, like civilians eager to return to their homes. Night has fallen and the vision of the convoy is impressive, the intermittent red lights following the curve around the bottom of a mountain a hundred meters beyond the highway. In other countries of the world the guerrillas would have already launched grenades or ambushed the convoy with dozens of deaths resulting. Here nothing happens. It's obvious that the Zapatistas don't want to shoot and desire to keep up a game of cat and mouse whose battlefield is the front page of several local newspapers, as well as newspapers from around the world. It's a great sound stage for a Hollywood film. This war in Chiapas, which has become fashionable to a certain extent in Europe and the United States, is atypical and engages in battles via the mass media. Publicity shots, celebrity grenades, world press bazookas.

In an uncovered truck a dozen men, women, children and dogs patiently withstand the long wait. The town of Las Limas is in complete darkness, the only thing visible a blinking antenna. They say everybody here is a Zapatista. But no one is afraid. On Dan's transistor we listen to the news on Radio France International and of course they're already talking about the federal army heading toward Simojovel as if it were war in the former Yugoslavia. The stars are clear and confused and fireflies flutter over the mountain. You can see a satellite pass through the sky: there's a fine little light moving through the stars at what must be an infernal speed, but from the ground it looks like something on a kid's video game. The dogs bark while we wait silently. The convoy continues the route once the trenches have been filled in by the soldiers. Later the same episode is repeated, but finally the last crossed trench gives way to Simojovel.

We cruise along until we reach the next check-point, where the military is already posted. A hundred meters farther on people stand on the sidewalks applauding and cheering the army, like a scene out of a film about the liberation of France. The stores are open, as well as the windows where beautiful village women in diaphanous skirts appear. Arriving to the plaza, Father Joel, accused of indoctrinating the Indians and inciting them to rise up against the whites since the outset of the Zapatista rebellion, and even more so now, begins a pre-Christmas *Posada,* a festival in opposition to the military deployment, with fireworks and hymns. He passes through the army lines as if nothing were going on.

On the main street everyone is outside celebrating. I don't see any Indians. They're all white, they might be as poor as the Indians, but the bottom line is they're white or *mestizo,* not "monolinguals" like those "masked dwarves" who emerge like ants from the humid mountains of Simojovel. The entire plaza is surrounded by military convoys, tanks and armored vehicles. Before the rebel church of the "red" parish priest Joel Padrón, who at first was said to be Subcomandante Marcos, men from the Federal Attorney General's office in blue bullet-proof vests take up position and flash their sawed-off shotguns as if suddenly hordes of Zapatistas or long-fanged killer vampire monks were about to emerge. The soldiers give money and candy to a few little white children who say they are happy to see them. A woman with Indian features who speaks Spanish very well, all greased up by a nice military tip, says it's "as if God has arrived." Her smile holds an incommensurable cynicism, the cynicism of an ancestral complicity of so many Mexicans with the ruling PRI regime. The merchants happily open their stores and accuse Joel Padrón of being the "little leader" of the Zapatistas. Someone says he has hurt the town, where he has lived for thirteen years. "He's filled the Indians' heads. Those Indians think they own everything and they enter the store all haughty asking for discounts because in the end they say it will all belong to them."

In the nicest store on the plaza where they sell appliances, the young heir disparages the priest and says hopefully the army won't leave, because then "we'll be at the mercy of those with guns." A young sympathetic French adventurer is there whom the heir introduces as his brother-in-law. Everybody in the family is happy to relate that one of their own is married to a French official, something that has being going on in these lands for a long time. During the nineteenth century in the Isthmus of Tehuantepec in the neighboring state of Oaxaca, an obligatory stop for merchant ships of the world and hundreds of adventurers who remained there, or in what is today Tabasco or the Yucatán, the Europeans married beautiful natives and started new lives which quickly turned them into rich landowners or prosperous merchants who no longer desired to return to the boring Old World. In his book *Travels through the Isthmus of Tehuantepec,* Father Charles Brasseur, translator of the Mayan codices, already relates in the mid-nineteenth century the rich life of these lands full of adventurers struck with marvel at the terrain here. A distinguished rancher, the happy father-in-law of the young Frenchman, offers us coffee and says that he is definitively a PRI supporter and is pleased by the arrival of the military. He's a short, robust white man, an important person in the community, the typical pro-government resident of the tropics dressed in a guayabera. In the mayor's office, the swarthy young state counselor wearing round eyeglasses, serious, but witty and intelligent, recognizes there was neither government nor authorities here before, but adds detachments will remain to protect the population. He reiterates there will be no friction with the Zapatistas. The town's wealthy residents approach the podium to greet this official of the status quo heading the convoy.

I walk around the plaza a couple times, listen to the rumors, watch the soldiers hide themselves. I ask for a couple eggs and tortillas at a food stand. I spoon on red chili sauce and listen to the news program *24 Hours* next to a detachment of federal judicial police armed to the teeth who lance insults at the screen when the genial writer Eraclio Zepeda appears, once a notable communist, a traveler to all the Eastern countries and now a member of the state government, which has prompted a furious reaction by his ex-*compañeros* on the left who have considered him a traitor since last December 8. I had just seen Zepeda in October in Bogotá at a theater packed with people who applauded him for the delightful oral tales he improvised.

A federal officer is surrounded by his little killer chickens with horrible faces who form the vast repressive machine charged with disappearing Indian rebels, helping out the "white guards," or death squads, maybe killing the transvestites in Tuxtla who, according to what they say around here, were eliminated after satisfying the pleasures of highly placed local officials. But despite the arms and such horrible faces I'm enchanted to be in this rustic diner, far from the Dunkin' Donuts, McDonald's, Kentucky Fried Chicken and Arby's of the city where I live, the place that long ago inspired Jack Kerouac's *Mexico City Blues.* Everything is tranquil here. The sounds of the insects in the jungle lull me. Midnight arrives and everything is calm. I walk alone through the streets, through the semitropical humidity that makes me recall villages in my land near the Magdalena River. Later I go sleep in a small hotel, Las Buganvilias, and I pass a peaceful night beneath the fan in a delicious sleep. The light has disappeared, the village remains in darkness.

Wednesday, December 21

I WAKE UP and go out to look for a toothbrush, toothpaste and disposable razor. The morning is cold and foggy. Next to the hotel is the provisional army camp where last night soldiers slept and on the street are still parked two tanks and two armored jeeps. It's curious to go out on the street like this and see those military vehicles washed so attentively by the soldiers. On the other street corner a fifty-year-old man waits nervously, startled to see those immense war vehicles stationed just ten meters away.

The store on the corner is closed and a veterinarian, a graduate from the capital named Hiparco Medino, engages me in conversation about Joel Padrón: the priest had gathered Indians on Medino's farm without seeking permission, he frequently passes by with menacing processions which make sales bad and people nervous. His uncle the storeowner hasn't opened up yet, but he agrees to unlock the gate and sell me what I need while venting against the Indians that according to him come in like they own the place and look him in the eyes like never before, for which he has to hide a lot of things of value. The well-outfitted merchant specializes in everything a campesino needs – rope, machetes, plates, brooms, rubber boots, belts, canteens, buckets, string, candies, paints, disinfectant. The man wants to show me everything, he wants me to come into his house and insists, completely disgusted, that it's all the fault of the priest who had "brainwashed the Indians, who you wouldn't believe used to be so peaceful and respectful." He is a quite different character than the notable and lucid cattleman from last night, the young Frenchman's father-in-law. This guy has the spirit of a greengrocer, he's a little lacking in brains, but his store fascinates me for such an array of objects that, like the rubber-tapping equipment, I haven't come across since childhood. I stay there a good while looking at the rustic tin lanterns, the old-fashioned straw brooms, the ropes and cords, the country hats and the thousands upon thousands of things covering the store walls in a never ending Baroque commercialism, a virtual fortune in merchandise. The man stands in the door looking in astonishment at the two enormous tanks on the corner as if he has seen a pair of dinosaurs come back to life. Poor man, I think as I leave his store with all the desperately needed articles for my bath at the Hotel Buganvilias.

After so many accusations from the shopkeepers and cattlemen, I go talk with the "monstrous" Joel Padrón, the celebrated "guerrilla priest" who was imprisoned for forty-nine days in the Cerro Hueco prison by the frightening ex-governor and ex-Minister of the Interior Patrocinio González Garrido for never proven accusations of robbery, damage to property, chicken theft, threats, provocation, associating with delinquents and gang members, conspiracy, possession of illegal military arms, and inciting to riot. His detention in September 1991 and the reaction displayed by the peasant population — thousands of Tzotzil, Tzeltal, Tojolabal, Chole, Mame and Zoque Indians from the region who demonstrated in the capital of Chiapas and successfully pressed for the priest's liberation, welcoming him with a fiesta when he was released from jail on the very same highway the convoy passed down last night — fore-warned the armed rebellion of January 1, 1994.

Padrón is a swarthy, athletic fifty-four-year-old priest who studied in Rome and speaks with great eloquence, always flashing a white-toothed smile and intelligent gaze that lends his entire being a charismatic air. Some of his most strident blessed female enemies in the town even tell us, without providing any proof, that he's a ladies man. No doubt they would like to have once sighed in the arms of the fit priest who receives me in his parish house where he lives with mentally retarded Indians and other beggars he feeds and lodges in messy, dusty rooms. He wears tennis shoes, jeans and a blue Levi's shirt. For him this is a battle between David and Goliath: a few impoverished children who protest with wooden rifles against centuries of oppression, facing down an immeasurable arrogant army of a government that doesn't want to listen to the "message" of those men "who stir tenderness, not fear." He laughs and says it's an honor for those poor Indians that they send an entire army against them. He hasn't even wanted to go see the military movement and asks me how many tanks and army trucks there are outside.

A little retarded guy laughs out loud and shows a coloring book to the priest, who patiently tells him to sit down, for he is talking to me now, after which the fellow concentrates quite awhile on drawing figures, occasionally bursting into laughter. Padrón doesn't conceal at all that he favors the Indians and distrusts the government, which he believes instead of trying to charge the indigenous people with criminal accusations should investigate and prosecute those guilty of their misery. A few minutes earlier the shop-keepers were telling me Padrón was guilty of putting such ideas into the heads of the Indians, the one who ruined private property and forced land holdings to be broken up.

They described him always surrounded by those Indians on processions into the nearby mountains. "Do you think a parish priest whose escort is this poor mentally retarded man heads a movement of such magnitude?" he asks and then laughs again beneath an enormous crystal chandelier, dusty and useless, hanging in a vestibule of creaking wood. Dampness inundates the old house and the hammers of workers resound in the distance.

Simojovel is now behind us. At the edge of town a few journalists who've arrived too late try to enter and see what's going on, but they're stuck in the half-full ditch. When they get through they will discern that the military vehicles aren't so visible now, discretely posted on side streets near the plaza, and that village life calmly goes on, but with the indigenous menace in the dense thicket covered by the fine morning fog smelling of fresh coffee beans. The coffee of San Simojovel. On the way back to San Cristóbal we stop to eat breakfast at an inn located in the Escopetazo, the so-called "Gun Shot." It reminds me of other places, like the road to a valley of La Vieja River, near Cartago, Colombia, places full of light and colorful flowers arrested in an idyllic, archaic time. A tall robust man waits on us and gives our orders for scrambled eggs to an old Indian woman; they take forever to make but taste delicious, and even more so when dressed with red chile sauce.

In the midst of all this I listen to the bellowing geese, frenzied, nervous, distrusting of the outlander passing by. I remember a trip I took to Cali with my father when I was nine in my Grandmother Mercedes' green Chrysler, a huge car with rounded forms, wide seats and a special smell that deepened with the afternoon heat in the Valley del Cauca. We descended into those fertile lands watered by the river coming from the cold heights, the region that was the setting for Jorge Isaacs' great Romantic novel *María,* published in 1867, the most widely read book of its time in Latin America. And there return those geese that ran after my father and me on a farm, images guarded in a family photo album, and I see him frozen a moment with a frank smile while we run down a little road in those distant years. Was it 1961 or 1962? There was a tense cease fire in Colombia's eternal endless violence; our family was doing well, the traces of violence seemed far away and we were still two decades from the country returning to its frightful cyclical horrors, crossed now with drug traffickers, right-wing extremists, guerrillas and the army. Within the capricious mechanism of memory, this present location immediately takes me to that modern Cali of the 1960s, with wide avenues and high buildings and photos from the past populated by the dead: father, mother, grandmother. Dan and Omar don't know I'm a prisoner of the past while the hot delicious coffee and the honking geese take me back thirty years to the Valley del Cuaca on one of my first journeys, one unforgettable and paradisiacal.

We are machines burdened with images from the past, our deaths are there and from time to time they greet us from their strange limbo, attracted by the color of certain flowers, the sounds of animals, some architectural trace. This inn, no doubt, was built around that period and looks like some of those we visited on that trip. I see my father, already fifty, dressed for once in casual clothes, my Catholic grandmother Mercedes with the distant gaze of old age, my sister, my mother and of course the boy I no longer am, with short hair, white jeans and a pale long-sleeved shirt standing next to a statue of Jorge Isaacs. It's not strange for us to be standing there next to the statue of this author who led a life of disaster and failure. His work impresses me because in it figure the black slaves brought to Colombia, their cultural imprint decisive in our history, with a music and vision of time and life so distinct from the Pre-Hispanic Indians. The love story between Efraín and María is still considered by Colombians our founding work of fiction, when decades after independence we finally ceased being a colony, when Bolívar and Santander were already dead, the heroes old men and the country on the road towards the future and progress. Jorge Isaacs, my father, Cali, the geese, a ten-year-old boy, a rebel priest who looks like a Latino Casanova: an absurd mixture provoked by chance at this roadside inn.

On the way back, almost at the end of the afternoon, we return again to San Andrés Larráinzar. Now the surprise is to find a trench two kilometers from town, dug that same afternoon by the Zapatistas to prevent vehicles from reaching the plaza. The atmosphere is tense, like yesterday, but now the plaza is everywhere full of people, Indians in their typical garb near the church, immutable men dressed in civilian clothes looking around, Tzotzil women with children in their arms standing in line near the mayor's office, dozens of dark men in hats under the arcades while a loudspeaker announces in Tzotzil that a Zapatista will be coming to explain the trenches and the take-over of the town. As hasn't happened for the last eleven months and twenty days, we know there won't be any shooting, at least for the moment; it's clear, though, that in any other Latin American country this would be the perfect scenario for a massacre.

A few minutes later the Zapatista appears, a campesino leader, maskless, and in a severe tone he expounds upon the reasons for their actions: a typical discourse from thirty years ago against monopolies, imperialism, bad government, poverty, the annexation of rural resources. It's clear that everyone agrees with him, except for the shopkeeper and a few local officials. The afternoon begins and the discourse continues. The rather poor shopkeeper, a rich woman here, of course disagrees with him and has called Tuxtla, so far unsuccessfully, for the army to come. Mist and cold fall over the sad plaza. The Zapatistas have taken the city and will emerge that night dressed in their military uniforms. Fog devours the town. We walk towards the trench where cars wait and a man in a ski mask is already guarding the pass. Behind us the Zapatista continues his interminable harangue before the residents' attentive, fixed, immutable gaze.

That night in the bar at the Santa Clara, I read and take notes while having a shot of vintage rum. This is the first night I feel settled in San Cristóbal, without the pressures of other trips as a correspondent. I've written up a lot of information and finally with the calm of a job done, I decide to relax. It's useless information because this situation is falling out of fashion, but in my case it's much better to jump on board at twilight. I'm a Colombian, a Latin American sitting at the bar, the only customer amidst all the crisis, while Television Azteca shows the successful Colombian soap opera *Café con aroma de mujer* and a newscast on the local channel transmits images of Subcomandante Marcos.

The waiters crowd around to tell me details about that mythical New Year just barely a year ago when that green-eyed hero in a ski mask appeared before the astonished tourists and natives. Through the windows the youngest and most excited waiter shows me where Marcos showed up, as if he were right beside him, as if he could feel his breath on that historic New Year he will surely describe to his grandchildren of the next century. As he recounts events he gets emotional and then disappears behind the bar, only to return worked up once more by the story, which I inquire into with great interest. He tells me the Marcos of that day isn't the Marcos of now, that he was a thinner, taller Marcos with green eyes like those of Jesus Christ, accompanied by his wife, a beautiful blond girl.

It's funny to see how myths are made: an enlightened man takes a risk, encounters a critical period in history, ventures into action and if he doesn't die trying he suddenly becomes an icon. I'm sure that if we could travel in a time machine and meet a few heroes from the past, we would end up disappointed. Tupac Amaru, José Antonio Galán, Bolívar, Martí, just to name a few of our own from Latin America, would seem like insignificant beings to us compared to their previous deification. But the creation of such gods is human nature, as these lands show in the steles dedicated by the Maya to their kings. In the northern part of this state, not far from here, is the splendorous Palenque, a Mayan city that shelters in one of its pyramids Pakal, as his liege called him, a monarch buried beneath a stone mass drawn with incomprehensible scenes of his acts and symbols of his functions. Imagine a statuesque and lucid king, although perhaps in real life he was a half-drunk, malnourished slob with a horrendous swollen belly, stupefied by spiritual smoke and drink, cruel, stinking and greasy.

And so on all through time we might try to unmask the many famous names we assume are great people, when maybe they were just rogues, killers, sell-outs, charlatans. A few heroes will have died without knowing they would later encapsulate a myth, and others will have claimed the valor of those under their command while they were getting drunk with scoundrels and whores. It's a matter of lucidity to always doubt heroes and gods, as well as flee from prophets and incorruptible wise men who scream the truth from mountaintops. How many of our own gods or heroes from the past were nothing more than crazy men on the loose, schizophrenics, paranoiacs, adventurers, men living in a sea of submission and ignorance? Nations, those terrible and monstrous inventions, feed off these semi-human images and their emblems in order to make idiots out of their subjects. The nation, the flag, the anthem, decisive battles, the liberator, the fraternity of the immeasurably pure defenders of the poor, martyred saints, great statesmen are all part of the biggest farce in history and we Latin Americans aren't the only ones with an exacerbated appetite for stories about crucified heroes.

What is it to be a Latin American? A lot of ink was spilled in the twentieth century about barbarism and civilization, Europe and the New World, universal and local culture, themes with which the natives of this land have tried to explain their strange mix. Thousand-year-old ruins flourish here, but we speak Spanish and for the last two centuries have nourished ourselves on the ideas of the French Enlightenment. There is no one racial type: we Latin Americans have faces of Spaniards and Moors, mulattos, mixed-bloods, Africans, some have the slanted eyes of the Orient, others the round faces of the Olmec, like those monumental heads more than 2000 years old found in Tabasco and Veracruz.

I have to recognize that I'm often assailed by this strange feeling of being a cultural Frankenstein. After six years residing in Paris, spending time as well all throughout Europe, the search for that "identity" and its recovery weren't something definite for me: I was born in Colombia and tried to flee it, from the terrible news that arrived to Europe from there during the '70s and '80s, the first decade tormented by a dirty war with tortured people, sectarian guerrillas who killed their own friends, implacable soldiers and a stubborn political class lacking in imagination. The second decade was overwhelmed by the madness of drug trafficking and its bombs and assassinations while the country looked for a way out, which unfortunately it has yet to find at this turn of the millenium. While abroad I have felt more than ever the pain of that Colombia through the anxiety of friends and relatives, convinced at times of the impossibility of escape, and one takes bitter refuge in that other world, choosing to devour instead its politics and literature and news. To return home would re-open the wound, embellish the pain. To be a Colombian, as Borges said, "is an act of faith," and it could be added that we begin to be Colombians when we pick up our passport: while traveling the Colombian affirms an eccentricity produced by a mixture of the world of African slaves and Indians and the Hispano-Arabic white race, a crazy blend of blood, music and literature.

But let's return to Mexico, one of Latin America's great countries, a world charged with pyramids, wars, virgins, temples, deserts, film, music, cuisine, the true concretion of the New World conflict from the Río Grande to Patagonia existing beside the powerful cultural crucible of the United States. Immersion in this Mexican labyrinth has brought other things into focus: Europe, the founding mother of our ideologies and intellectual madness, much more transparent from here the perception of its culture, its history, its advances and setbacks, its holocausts and festivals, its thousand-year-old temples and futuristic avenues; and the land of my birth, the place of childhood and youth, Colombia, as having truly decided to try to understand its own genocide while still hanging onto a ritualistic and congenital violence, passing through a strange modernity with its own risks. The Aztecs performed horrible sacrifices atop their pyramids, we do our own in the streets with gunfire.

It was like a vision: the Colombia I recently visited is another country from the one I left twenty years ago. On one hand it desires to be, think, write, relate and recuperate its past and confront its future in a febrile night life full of ideas and art and Expressionist exuberance, and on the other it continues to be made dull and stupid by the dictatorship of the mass media enthroned like pagan gods, and by a general social *arrivisme.* At the same time, beloved Europe constructs and destroys itself between conflicts and insecurities. It's as if suddenly in certain Latin American sectors we stopped being those clumsy little kids, a bit conflicted and bitter, and our generation no longer needed to pirouette and juggle just to exist, while Europe, with its mid-century holocaust, seems to lose the fragile security of progress and post-war wealth while lurking ghosts eat away at it. I see on one side a Europe full of racial conflicts, unemployment, economic fragility, poverty, uncertain about integration, on the way toward underdevelopment, its monsters still alive, and on the other a Latin America sure of its faults and its qualities, a wide chaotic specter of some twenty nations with lucid, electric generations nourished on a great cultural century. And on the world stage I see a fearful and indecisive United States, its streets full of poverty and racial conflicts, its great dream worm-eaten and ready to fall into decay.

The brief episode of ideological fashions in the '60s and '70s gave way to an intellectual generation in Latin America with a delicious cynicism that captures the forces of its millenary past without making them into gods: modernism, the avant-guard, regionalism, humanism, the narrative "boom," the poetic apogees of recent decades. We live with them but without the oppositions, interferences and distrust of the Cold War that finally sank in 1989.

Here, sitting in a bar in San Cristóbal de las Casas, I see things much more clearly than I did twenty years ago. I look with a certain optimism at the path our culture is taking, a most important thing to do, for fools and political thieves pass but cultures go on. I believe we are discovering that we can live without the accelerated ambition of progress, with neither the dogma of neoliberalism nor the messianic geniuses coming from an impossibly happy world. But will our politicians ever learn this? We are this colored chaos, sometimes terrible and sometimes possessing the overwhelming beauty which Simón Bolívar describes in his famous *Letter from Jamaica.* We just have to look around to know and understand ourselves. Our reality was here and we didn't see it, and for that reason we sought it out desperately in magic realism and in revolutionary dreams or the authoritarian, chimerical First World. We are neither better nor worse: we are. We shine in our pyramids and golden burial mounds, in the rich, vast, unending natural world, in the idiom of an entire hemisphere charged with dialects past and present, in our streets and books of a living Spanish language, in our cities full of intense music, flavors, hates and affections, lies and certainties: prophecies and magic in the strict and happy sense of the word.

I perceive all this here with unaccustomed force: I'm a Latin American writer sitting at a bar with an excellent glass of rum, "so ancient and so modern," as the great Rubén Darío said a hundred years ago. Here is my father the liberal and radical Jacobean, my conservative, Catholic praying grandmother; the guerrilla uncle, my poet brother, the first entrepreneur, the vampire relative, the murderer and the tender dreamer, Jorge Luis Borges and Julio Cortázar, Enrique Molina and Vicente Gerbasi, Rómulo Gallegos and José Eustasio Rivera, Alejo Carpentier and Miguel Ángel Asturias, Pedro Infante and Carlos Gardel, Libertad Lamarque and María Félix. An unequalled elaborate tapestry which no doubt will be reproduced generation after generation. In a hundred years this list of variations will sound old-fashioned and those names will be replaced by others from this Latin America which is at heart entertaining, endless, generous and cruel, carnivalesque and ridiculous, a delicious cabaret spectacle.

We are alive on our continent: there is color, parties, sex, words, poetry, adventures, death, lies, masks, imagination, hypnotism, magic, landscapes, the Baroque, sweetness, chili peppers, *merecumbé, salsa, currulao, cumbia,* desire, men wielding knives, thieves, beggars, strongmen. We are the continent of desire. We are always at a rolling boil. We have the soul of immigrants and colonizers. We founded cities and regions. The poor still hold festivals, from the Book of Job to *Blade Runner.* Isn't that preferable to the rigid puritan solitude of many cities and provinces of the poorly named First World, so coveted by our technocrats, where corruption and poverty also exist? Because the great farce of free enterprise and market economics is that indeed investors in the stock market cheat and don't accept losing. Those on the bottom always end up paying, whether here or in New York. We used to want to be like the boring Soviet Union of gray-suited Stalinists, the frightful China of Mao Zedong or the precarious Cuba of Fidel Castro; and now the dictatorship of businessmen and accountants -- what witless beings! -- wants to convert us into a great factory of puritan zombies.

Thursday, December 22

AT DAWN we leave in a white pick-up truck and head towards the road block at Las Margaritas, hoping to enter Zapatista territory and reach Guadalupe Tepeyac, the bastion of Subcomandante Marcos. Driving is a young Mexican photographer nicknamed Indiana Jones who four years ago, right after my father died, took a photo of me for a book I wrote where I pose with the desolate expression of a recently abandoned orphan. Nothing more terrible than the death of the father. Suddenly man sees himself thrown out onto the street, slapped in the face by that certain ineluctable end. It's a knife in the soul whose scars take a long time to heal. The gaze fixes on nothing and the body feels like a piece of something bigger cut adrift, as if a limb has been cut off.

On this trip with Indiana Jones I see the first bloody settings of last year's battles. When this Zapatista rebellion erupted January 1, 1994, I stayed in the Mexico City newsroom in the Latin American Tower, the Aztec Empire State Building constructed in 1954. From that date on we spent many hectic months writing thousands and thousands of wires and articles about the Zapatistas, the assassination in March of Luis Donaldo Colosio, the official candidate for president, the August elections, the ensuing crimes and changes and the new president taking office, but during the entire year I never set foot in Chiapas. In Mexico City — that infernal lamentation of cars and people: cities within cities and countries within countries, wealthy neighborhoods with walled houses and lost slums that take form in just a few years upon ancient lakes or misbegotten hills; lowlifes, Indians, executives in Armani suits, ranchers in cowboy hats, mariachis, gang bangers, punk rockers, Northerners, hot-blooded men, tough sons of bitches, spoiled rich kids in luxury autos, beer halls, cantinas, *pulquerías,* exclusive discotheques, strip clubs with lap dancers, tropical tea rooms — there were demonstrations, great palace intrigues, obscure changes in the streets.

In a press agency you become a kind of robot with flashing lights. There is a certain addiction to computers, to the wires coming in about different topics and amidst the local buzz you find on the screen every sort of strange information from the most distant corners of the world, like the scientific news about the discovery of the Smilaun man in the Tyrolean Alps or the new cosmic revelations of the Hubbell telescope being adjusted for a special mission, the discoveries of ancient Greek, Phoenician or Roman ships in the waters of the Mediterranean full of flasks and vessels, or galleons in the Caribbean full of treasure chests and ingots of gold. This side of journalism seems warmer and more human to me, news of greater permanency that doesn't age like sterile politics, economics and sports. Journalism enters the twenty-first century in a great pathological crisis, a cold infernal machine that distances man from his true nature, a self-devouring hysteria of useless information.

For months San Cristóbal de las Casas was invaded by hundreds and hundreds of journalists, first to cover the unimaginable combat in January and later during the negotiations in February and March of 1994. The vast majority were misplaced foreigners eager for tropical folk lore and hundreds of free-lancers of every hue. In the press room set up for months on Diego de Mazariegos came and went unattributed rumors. A few dull correspondents pretended they were onto a great story without knowing this was a paper war. No doubt most of them wouldn't have dared tour the sordid massacres in some African country or villages wiped out by howitzers and mortars in the former Yugoslavia, or bloody and terrifying Chechnya during its Siberian winter.

While events were taking place in San Cristóbal, Mexico City saw a lot of movement and many people thought that the official party, the PRI, was on the point of collapsing and finally the defeats occurring over the last several years in the East would be reflected in a domino affect in this country, dominated throughout the century by one sole party, the "philanthropic ogre" as Octavio Paz called it in one political essay.

January 12, for example, young people and members of the opposition protested against the government in a mass demonstration to end the war and the massacre of the Indians. It was a demonstration charged with youthful energy, and we all know it is youth who still protest with enthusiasm, before they're devoured by adulthood and its sad doldrums and ignominious struggle to earn a living. The walls on Madero Avenue were completely covered by signs in favor of Marcos and the EZLN, and fast food restaurant managers saw their windows stained with graffiti. As well the walls of the National Palace were covered by banners and the front wooden portal with an enormous drawing of Che Guevara, who emerged from the ruins of the socialist dream to be hoisted aloft by kids who weren't yet born the day he died. Around dawn, the authorities brought out thousands of workers to erase the traces of the rebellion and the walls were made newly clean, as if nothing had happened. In Mexico it's impressive how demonstrations, even the most heated, calmly take place and at the end of the parade follow sanitation workers, escorted in turn by police patrols, who clean up the garbage left by the demonstrators and the traces of their mobilization.

But since the agitated days of 1988, when the opposition presidential candidate Cuauhtémoc Cárdenas probably won the election but his victory wasn't recognized, I hadn't seen such a decided and enthusiastic demonstration. Ministers were falling and Colosio, the candidate of the country's nearly sole party, hadn't garnered much enthusiasm; he was later killed and a new candidate was named, Ernesto Zedillo, a rather opaque personality, the typical Latin American with a diploma from an American university, dry and uninterested in the arts, who holds power throughout the continent.

Everything pointed to a key year in Mexico's history and many outside analysts accepted this illusion, not knowing that in the 1994 elections the great majority of the population — young and old, demonstrators and non-demonstrators — would approve with millions of votes a referendum to let the all-powerful party continue and so "betray" the poor and enthusiastic Marcos and his thousand diminutive followers. The Mexican public turned its back on the dream of rebellion and preferred to maintain its immobile master. It was scared to kill daddy. The tons of paper and ink used to talk about the inevitable "change" of the Mexican political system vanished into thin air. We shouldn't judge them, they were probably right. Masochism is natural to most peoples and in this case it's obvious the pre-Hispanic ritual of circularity and recurring fire was still alive. For the patriarchal party to fall would break the chain of history, to knock down the columns of Mexican cosmology.

The spectacular *happening* headed by Marcos in touristic San Cristóbal had a series of ingredients that facilitated his media success. After taking the initial risk, the Zapatistas had no more need for bullets; any declaration, movement, spectacle was enough to attract journalists anywhere. Chiapas became a necessary news item with Indians of distinct ethnic groups, marginalized priests, nearby Mayan ruins, dreamy landscapes, masked guerillas, sad harp music, ancestral dances, wicked white ranchers in cowboy hats out of some old movie, nuns and nurses menaced and besieged for helping the Indians, future Mother Teresas under the dog day sun, an all-powerful Army held in check by journalists, risk-taking tourists, Europeans and North Americans wishing they were the new Indiana Jones.

Those of us born during the times of revolutionary and hippie dreams, who grew up amidst peace signs and free love and the struggle against exploitation, those of us who have defended the cause of Indians, blacks, gays, find ourselves in familiar territory here in San Cristóbal de las Casas, Chiapas, glued together in the last half-decade of the twentieth century for a neo-hippie generation sick of years dominated by yuppies with styled hair and double-breasted suits. In the plaza of San Cristóbal de las Casas you don't see middle-aged tourists complaining about a chipped coffee cup or the lack of bottled water or people who wouldn't dare stray from the luxury hotels on plastic beaches like Cancún or Ixtapa, those jewels of Mexican modernity. On the contrary, these are long-haired boys and girls with back packs and army boots looking for something else, a kind of ideological tourism, or old Catholics and leftists who come to wash clean their consciences. People in general who because of their Franciscan innocence cause goose bumps in the rational, complicit intellectual rungs of the powerful. The day this delirium comes to an end will be sorrowful.

The journalists, the new hippies, the few rebels fighting against the "perfect dictatorship," the Christians nostalgic for Liberation Theology will all mourn. Where are they going to find another guerrilla movement as original and in a country so much on the radar screen, the country of the Mayans and the Aztecs, of Malcolm Lowry, Burroughs and Kerouac, of Trotsky and Artaud, of Dolores del Río and Augustín Lara? A non-Marxist guerrilla movement that doesn't seek power and moreover only kills with words?

I'm thinking all this over while Indiana Jones flies along the road and points out mythic places of Chiapanecan achievement. We come to the big boring town of Comitán. Beyond Las Margaritas, we finally reach the well-known military roadblock where for the entire first year who ever had the dream of seeing Marcos or Ramona or Tacho or Moisés could pass into rebel territory. But during this new escalade things are tense. The military had relaxed its guard and the astute Zapatistas broke through the blockade after months of inactivity, right before Christmas, and now go around everywhere causing problems, digging trenches and felling trees on the highways, setting up unexpected check points and giving speeches in public plazas. The peaceful villagers suddenly become Zapatistas only by putting on their black ski masks and later change back into discrete Indians with impenetrable gazes. The military wants to put an end to them, but world attention prevents it. The damn fad of human rights has finally arrived to Mexico and the thugs and assassins have to control themselves.

For centuries colonial governments, republicans, and institutional revolutionaries killed Indians on the spot and almost nobody paid any attention. A famous book, *Barbarous Mexico*, relates the horrors of the Porfirio Díaz regime. It was written by a young journalist at the beginning of the twentieth century named John Kenneth Turner, who passed himself off as an investor and so directly witnessed the exploitation in the countryside, on plantations and in mines. He says something that can applied with a few changes to the current situation, one often endorsed by the people themselves with a reverent, legitimizing complicity.

Turner discovers that "the true Mexico is a country where neither the Constitution nor laws are obeyed…without political liberty, without free speech, without a free press, without a judicial system…a land where the people are poor because they have no rights, where slavery exists for hundreds of thousands of people." He describes the selling of political positions and the lack of a fair and transparent electoral process, but also comes to believe that "Mexicans of all classes and affiliations agree that their country is on the point of beginning a revolution in favor of democracy."

This book, published in 1910 and attacked by the government and the exploiters as being part of a foreign conspiracy against the nation, demonstrates that today's vituperative idealists belong to this old current who today demonstrate to the world that the current *Criollo* technocrats in power differ little from the "scientifics" of Porfirio Díaz. Marcos and the Zapatistas made a joke out of those young yuppie officials who over the years have unceasingly repeated their dogmas and dismissed those who opposed them as ignorant and anachronistic.

On various occasions — at preparatory meetings for the North American Free Trade Agreements in Zacatecas and Acapulco, or GATT in Puerto Vallarta — I witnessed the flowery catechism of free market ideology with its infallible terms taught to its adoring acolytes at US universities: "competitiveness," "First World," "viability," "cost/benefit analysis," among much other jargon. What is the difference between the priests of Marxist totalitarianism and those of capitalist totalitarianism? In place of the paradise of Catholics and socialists, these lay priests preach about a First World paradise: cities full of supermarkets and fast food outlets, freeways with the latest automobiles, buildings of transparent glass, gigantic consumer shopping malls, their millions of residents scurrying about like little ants, undermined by shiny and inexhaustible credit cards, a world of beaches with air-conditioned five-star hotels inhabited by dyed blondes with perfect teeth and bodies, and behind them filthy little stands of Mexican tacos, anachronistic *ranchera* music, Baroque churches and markets offering Indian trinkets, inhabited by low-lifes who no doubt are to those functionaries a dead weight in the modernization of the country.

Such an ideology has been sprinkled like dust over the entire continent and it was even said that Mexican yuppies were leading the rest of us Latin Americans by the hand toward the First World paradise. The world press pointed them out with distinction, they appeared on the front pages of newspapers and in newsmagazines, they tried to talk the least amount possible in anachronistic Spanish, giving press conferences in every language except that of their own country. For years we put up with those monstrous personages who knelt in the most ignominious manner possible before George Bush and Bill Clinton's trade representatives, and later were applauded by a series of presidents throughout the Americas who acted like characters from some operetta, eager to be let into the club. Whoever didn't agree with a "free market economy that generates well-paying salaries" was arrogantly refuted. Radio and television dedicated hour after hour reporting on movements and prices in the stock market and advised the audience on lucrative investments, while millions of the t.v. watchers and radio listeners were only poor zombies without a peso in their pockets, praying grandmothers, hungry construction workers, thirsty day laborers, strangled bitter members of the middle-class.

Little was the difference between the totalitarian discourse of communist countries with their dogmas and heroes and the incessant, schizophrenic discourse of the neo-liberal economic commentators who sprang up like mushrooms. While free market Big Brother was talking, the migrating capitalists, vampires with neither country nor law, sucked the resources out of the country and local fat cats made secret deals and transferred their money. After hearing about another devaluation of the peso, I am sure that the real phase of history is beginning, a new nightmare, and that this skirmish in Chiapas arrives like a bucket of cold water suddenly thrown into the face of the religion of neo-liberalism which had asserted, like Stalin did in his time, that history ended with its triumph. No doubt the free market and capitalism, whose development have brought great advances to mankind along with ominous dangers, have their qualities. I don't want to fall into some myopic intransigent discourse that sees all evil on one side.

The world has no order. The most spectacular magician couldn't solve the lack of equality nor immunize man so he would limit his ambition and compulsion for power, authority, violence and arbitrariness. Wherever there is a group of men, one of them will always want to take advantage of the others and once on the throne, like Fidel Castro and so many others, will try to outlast in years with their own dictatorship the tyranny they removed. The sympathetic hero will grasp onto power with more rage and passion than his predecessors and will even send his best friends to the firing squad in order to hang onto power. Any person of average intelligence knows this has been the law of humanity ever since it began populating the planet. But from time to time we have to relive that history, to repeat it in order not to forget it. Poets have as their marvelous mission rebellion, subversion, incredulity in face of human actions. The greatest thing about a hero is his defeat, the worst his triumph: the pure state of the hero is his endless struggle.

The poet must celebrate the discomfort of the powerful, in this case the ideology of capital in its most recent version of the privateer being challenged by the weak. The strength of this vagabond Marcos stems from him spoiling the technocratic party that marked the beginning of NAFTA, directing the cameras of the press instead toward the forgotten Indians hidden in San In-the-Middle-of-Nowhere. A year after the uprising, the lid has been taken off the myth of that infallible "Mexican miracle" of belonging to the First World, the fictitious myth of other Latin American countries whose scream will soon be heard as well.

But let's get back to the trip. When we reach the roadblock situated in a paradisiacal location, Colonel Lara, who they say used to joke around with the tourists, sits tensely at a tent in the middle of the military post. This very day they have prohibited passage to everyone and we are the first ones turned away. The army is on alert and no doubt Lara knows his colleagues are going to enter Yajalón, beyond Simojovel, and then San Andrés Larráinzar. Perhaps they want to go all the way to Guadalupe Tepeyac, the bastion of Marcos, and end this problem once and for all. He tells us that only the Red Cross can pass. It is useless to try convincing him otherwise. "It's for your own safety," he says. "Your life would be in danger," he adds while handing us back our identifications. For the moment the party is over.

We head back full speed to San Cristóbal, but turn off toward Los Llanos and head over to Ocosingo and try entering Zapatista territory through the other bastion of San Miguel. Passing through Rancho Nuevo, Indiana Jones shows me the place where the first Zapatistas were machine-gunned during that horrible January. I remember the first color photos appearing on the computer screen which shook all of us at the press agency: Indians in red bandanas bleeding next to a minibus sprayed with machine-gun fire, bodies sprawled on the green grass and thrown onto the highway. During those days Mexico was on edge. Suddenly the phantom of the Zapatista revolution from the beginning of the century appeared, the specters of men hung from lamp posts or trees near the train stations, as Octavio Paz relates in one of his memoirs, returned by the thousands. The silence of those killed before a firing squad resounded in the distance, women assaulted and raped, cruel local political bosses wielding power. Those photographed episodes traumatized the capital's middle-class, terrorized even more by a bomb found at University Plaza, a typical modern shopping center, placed there by who knows what obscure force.

The tranquility of the place is impressive. Moreover the highway is perfect, recently asphalted, the car slipping and sliding from time to time from our speed. A bit further on appears a jail recently liberated by the Zapatistas, now an empty white elephant with desolate guard towers and broken windows. Another blow from the Zapatista troops. Familiar names like Teopisca, Amatenango del Valle, Chilón, Huistán, Ejido López Mateos, Oxchuc, Altamirano and Ocosingo, where the massacre in the market occurred and Zapatistas were shot with their hands tied behind their backs. This last place brings to mind macabre photos of the exhumation of Indian corpses in January of 1994.

Later the wide-open highway looms, farther on blocked by enormous tree trunks placed there by the rebels, cut down with powerful chainsaws to impede the imminent invasion by federal troops. An old bus stops there, and a few peasants get off with their possessions and clamber over the trunks on the way back to their communities under the control of the Zapatista government. I climb a tree and listen to the familiar sounds of the mountain. It's impossible to enter the land of the "faceless men." We fly back through scenery recorded now in my memory, and I try to discern in the silence the horrors of a year ago.

Tonight, taking refuge before the former Convent of Santo Domingo, I recall the demonstrations in Bogotá during my youth when the army took over the National University: the perilous battle of young people against the body of the mounted armed forces, a rather normal event everywhere in the world; it even appears in Flaubert's *Sentimental Education*, when the dream wasn't socialism but the republic, and in the work of Dostoievsky with his marvelous conspirators. It's strange that men of great intelligence, Latin American intellectuals who have created splendid works, manage to lose perspective of time and, dedicated to analyzing what is happening now on this continent and throughout the world according to their dogma, don't see the ebb and flow of the generations.

The idea of the end of history attempts to legitimize that immobility: the robots of Fritz Lang's *Metropolis* or those in Orwell's *1984* detained in a perfect cold-blooded emotionless world, a world of mannequins, well-oiled androids detained in a desolate, timeless ambience. Some of those intellectuals hurried to pass sentence on the rebels in Chiapas without hearing them out, without taking time to analyze things, without trying to understand the reasons behind the problems that obviously don't reside in the intrinsic evil of a few white adventurers who try to deceive the poor.

This is the sad sectarianism of the middle and upper classes of the Americas, opposed out of hand to that strange world, to the other, to the different, to the half-breed, to the low-life, to the desolate. For the white middle-class that has killed off the youthfulness it once possessed, it is inexplicable that there are people who speak other languages or dialects and don't want to enter the First World of McDonald's and luxury shopping malls, the world of that sterile "pure" democracy that isn't quite so pure here and doesn't stand up to intense analysis. Who are those Indians? What do they smell like? What are their dreams? To what do they aspire? How do they talk? What do they eat and what do they think, the broken, the dregs of society, the Indians? Do they have a soul? Are they human beings? Are they rational beings? These questions can be asked in turn about millions and millions of displaced beings in the awful Latin American apartheid that those intellectuals still can't see, blinded as they are by the catechism of progress.

Francis Picabia said "the brain is round so ideas can circulate," but in the Americas the polarization of the last years has put an end to the dialogue, the discussion, the civilized debate between yesterday's sectarian leftists, who now have begun to fade away, and the current chiefs of the "market economy" composed of the mass media and the grand capitalists. When those Indians suddenly demonstrated in the free market project's model country, these intellectuals wanted to dogmatically label them as old Marxists, killers, deluded people intoxicated by ideology, mercenaries guided by Argentines or Central Americans, children of Stalin. Those dirty decrepit Indians who don't eat hamburgers or Campbell soup deserve only our words of contempt for having spoiled NAFTA's party. Whoever stopped a moment to try dispassionately to understand, to dive into, to grasp onto the origins of the Zapatistas was immediately classified as a nostalgic leftist, a reader of Lenin or Mao. To the Cuban dictator Castro's "Revolution or Death," they offered "Free Market or Death."

I move now to Paris, 1975. I had left behind the violent demonstrations of Bogotá and the sinister leftist sects that looked at us with contempt for our love of literature. We were still living under the glare of the 1968 rebellion, corralled off at the University of Paris-Vincennes in corridors smelling of fried *merguez* and Arab pastries, teeming with Africans, Latin Americans, including gay or wrong-thinking Cubans persecuted by Castro, French and exiled European rebels. Through those Vincennes hallways passed Foucault, Deleuze, Guattari, Pasolini, André Gunder Frank, Samir Amin, René Schérer, Alfredo Bryce Echenique, Saul Yurkievich, Herbert Marcuse, Jacque Lacan and so many others who came together during those years.

I remember clearly a demonstration I joined that year of 1975: in a little studio apartment at 25 rue Moret we listened to the call of the old man Sartre to demonstrate against the Spanish dictator Francisco Franco, whom he called a *salaud latin,* and demand that several young rebels not be executed by the vile noose. A multitudinous manifestation left the Parc Monceau, passed down the Champs Elysée and crossed north to the Place de Concorde. There were groups of diverse origins, all infuriated at the tyrant, and in the end everything degenerated into a pitched battle with several buildings of the Spanish government in Paris set on fire, with even an assault on the famous restaurant Maxim's and other confrontations with authorities in a dance of paving stones reminiscent of 1968.

That festival of rebellion I experienced at twenty-one remains in my memory because it demonstrates the giving and open nature of youth as it confronts tyranny. Some people were still angry at André Malraux, who had headed a counter-demonstration down the Champs Elysées against the impossible triumph of that countercultural madness. He perhaps had his reasons at the twilight of his long and fruitful life, but now, at the turn of the millenium, there is no doubt those movements contributed to generating today's diverse and tolerant thought that goes beyond the sad dogmas and trenches of the Cold War. No doubt Malraux, who fought against fascism in Spain as a youth had listened, just a year before his death, with bother and disdain to those ragged rebels. Did we understand him in his old age? Will we also understand that some old men and their young hit men from our own Latin America are incapable of understanding that this is our world, and as Galileo once said, "And yet, it moves"? The generation that ran through the streets of Paris wasn't looking for power but the right to protest, so that others — the strange, the unbalanced, the marginalized, the disposable — might speak with their own voice.

In a Latin America lacking statesmen, the intellectuals, poets and novelists are obliged to occupy the space of language and become political prophets, not in order to seek power, but because there is and there must be the right to criticize, to debate, to listen to the other outside the context of the old Cold War, a phenomenon which still generates the ignorant and insensible style of thinking about the world's problems of today's technocrats and their lettered buffoons, a period still present in some minds like a long and dirty obsession. In this vast Latin American cauldron we must abandon a university-educated sophistry and stop a moment to consider with new strategies our past, present and future.

The effect of the Cold War has been so devastating over the last three or four decades that Latin Americans have forgotten how to think like their great essayists of the first half of the twentieth century. Those old writers who so generously communicated between different countries, from Mexico City to Montevideo and Buenos Aires, from

Santiago to Caracas, Lima and Bogotá, from Havana and Guatemala City to New York and Paris, who placed the first stones of reflection about the different mixes within the Latin American world, are an example for these accelerated times. People talk about the postmodern, cosmopolitan world, the breaking of national boundaries (which, moreover, others earlier have reflected upon), but this shouldn't prevent us from trying to situate ourselves in the camp of our Spanish language as well as in our culture crossed with pyramids, vice royal palaces, republican capitals and great housing projects inspired by Le Corbusier.

The *boom* years and the exacerbation provoked by Castro's dreams in Cuba led us toward a facile Latin Americanism, a caricature that undervalued the past and left in the closet modernists like Rubén Darío and Herrera y Reissig, the poetic avant-garde of Huidobro, the earthy atmosphere of Rivera and Gallegos and the many writings of Alfonso Reyes and Henríquez Ureña. As well were left behind, replaced by military dictators and technocrats, the old and anachronistic politicians schooled in Latin and Greek. It would be healthy to rebuild bridges with those people forgotten in the pantheons of illustrious men: their voice might be more useful for us than journalistic clamoring and tiring supermarkets. The best seller and journalism, the badly named "sciences of communication," now confiscate the space of thought. Speed prevents us from locating the movements of the tectonic plates that underlie this Tower of Babel. Obviously we live in a "globalized" world, but we also have a past with voices and knowledge that few listen to or try to imagine.

Sitting in a plaza facing the church of Santo Domingo, in cold San Cristóbal de las Casas, I see it clearly: we are on the eve of a new millenium and here are those Indians who speak their own language and don't eat hamburgers, and there are the bell towers of ancient Christianity far from Hollywood. There is silence, wind, no television. Fortunately journalists are nowhere around, speeding along heading towards nowhere: a centuries-old former convent isn't news.

Friday, December 23

"BUY A RAMONA and a Marcos from me," says the little Indian girl with lank braided hair, big eyes, a prominent nose and dark, citrine skin. "Buy them both from me, they're Ramona and Marcos," she says referring to two of the heroes sanctified by popular imagination through these little masked cloth dolls. "Buy a Ramona and a Marcos from me, buy a Ramona and a Marcos from me," insists the little girl, now accompanied by another ten kids offering colored bracelets, vests, bags and other souvenirs. Thousands of tourists have bought entire armies of those rustic dolls, impressive just to look at with their little thread eyes, indecipherable ski masks, wooden rifles and cartridge belts full of bullets. Ramona sprang into being a local celebrity during the peace talks in March when the guerrillas returned to dialogue and, protected during their stay in the cathedral by Samuel Ruiz, were the object of incessant photo sessions and press conferences. That diminutive, robust young woman was always beside Marcos and since then has remained in the memory of local artisans. Her figure is reproduced and she has become the archetype of the Zapatista woman. Just a few years later she will die of cancer.

There is no news to report and so I become another tourist. Buy today's newspapers, visit the two or three bookstores in the city, which certainly have a nicely nourished selection. Have a gin and tonic at some hotel on the Zócalo, take a walk by the Cathedral. At times I wonder what will happen with the words of this diary. If I don't destroy them I will have the permanent temptation to publish them and add to the fattening list of books inspired by Chiapas. I've heard about a book published in Barcelona, another in France, besides another dozen best sellers made on the fly. There have recently emerged biographics of Marcos, proclamations and letters of the *Subcomandante,* luxurious photographic editions, anthologies and compilations of writings, recompilations of anthropological and social essays. But I'm not interested in writing these words with the pretension of giving testimony about a war that is not a war in the conventional sense but a theater of shadows and gestures. In this case there is the mere coincidence that the correspondent is first of all a poet, a writer, a novelist, the person for whom landscapes, facts, visions, and news take on other dimensions. I'm almost sure that among the mass of reporters and photographers who await some press conference and brandish their cellular phones in the courthouse to talk with their station chiefs at their offices in the capital, few look beyond their sad, petty task. If these words have emerged it's from the literary need to flee from the wires and the press and invoke something else.

Poets and writers, even if they know how to do their work better than journalists, will always be suspect in the eyes of the latter, perceived as intruders, strange beings, dreamers: their gaze begins where that of others ends. Journalists can't stand them for the simple reason that they themselves are basically beans to be counted by the merchants of news. And so the writer, the poet, the reader, is a true rival whose eyes they don't dare look into. It doesn't make me uncomfortable to say that the poet among journalists is a god. And if I write this text, whether or not I destroy it later, it's out of an aesthetic, literary need. It could have surfaced somewhere else. Instead of being here I could have taken a first voyage to Asia, to the ends of the earth, and describe day after day the emerging feelings, ideas, facts. In Greenland, in Ulan Bator, in Iceland, in Madagascar, in Patagonia. While traveling, the writer is assaulted by thousands of things: visions, sensations, sorrows, joys, poetry, dreams; old lovers appear, or those who weren't, the voices of dead ancestors are heard and you try to reconstruct those faces to outline a family tree; sitting in a plaza you re-order memories or write post cards, see bodies that remind us of other bodies or faces that remind us of other faces, weave momentary relationships that later dissolve into smoke. That is what this diary is trying to do: allow ideas and colors, memories and landscapes to germinate and bud, call forth ghosts, capture passers-by, not let escape a sole aroma I smell, a sole woman I see, a sole church bell I hear.

That's what our beloved Montaigne did in his *Essays* and in a one of my favorite books, *Voyage to Italy,* that I read while awaiting the birth of my daughter Oriana in a hospital in Mexico City's Colonia Roma on August 29, 1984. I love to read the diaries of writers and am reminded of two which left their mark on me, those of Virginia Woolf and Cesare Pavese, both tormented, suicidal beings, authors who desired to explore the mystery of their creation. I enjoy the diaries of voyages by great navigators like Marco Polo, Pigafetta, Alvar Núñez Cabeza de Vaca's *Shipwrecked,* the famous *Historias trágicas-marítimas* by Portuguese sailors, the writings of Bougainville, Humboldt, Darwin, and Charles Brasseur, translator of the *Popol Vuh* whose *Voyage through the Isthmus of Tehuantepec* I adore.

The list of those testimonies about life is endless. I regret that in these times we've lost the possibility for adventure. Wherever you go you find the same hotels, identical television channels, international magazines and news programs that keep us informed for the good or the bad about what's going on in the world. It's quite difficult for a hurricane or a typhoon to cast us off as shipwrecks so that we end up wandering lost for years as did Alvar Núñez among fierce tribes, among *barbarians* as the natives were called by those European voyagers who foundered on the coasts of Africa in the fifteenth and sixteenth centuries. It's impossible now to become a prisoner of cannibals or encounter a panther or a Bengal tiger, species on the verge of extinction. I raise my Heineken beer; I might like a Guinness or a Rolling Rock, alternative flavors to the many delicious Mexican beers which I will recall nostalgically some day when I'm no longer living in this country, although undoubtedly I'll be able to find them anywhere.

What worries me most now is what lays hidden in diaries: how much of what they contain is unsayable? A favorite phrase of André Malraux comes to mind that I found in one of his delicious *Antimemoires*: "Il est admis que la verité d'un homme, c'est d'abord ce qu'il cache" — it's obvious that the truth of a man is first of all what he hides. And indeed what reaches us about famous men is barely a mutilated part of the truth. What we think about the people who surround us, the sordid worlds we visit, the bodies we desire and possess, the subtle hatreds, the humiliating disasters, the lies, the masks, the traps, the envy, all those qualities left out of statues (although figures like Sade, Casanova, Henry Miller, Charles Bukowski, Jean Genet and Anaïs Nin remain in history as wicked transgressors) are just the polished surface of the truth.

Among the books I've brought along with me is a Colombian classic by Fernando González, *Voyage on foot,* widely read by my father's generation and still successfully republished. One December the iconoclastic thirty-three-year-old born in 1895 leaves Medellín to head through the mountains on foot in company of his friend Benjamín Correa with the goal of passing through Manizales and later reaching the sea at Buenaventura. González, a very discomfiting author in Colombia at that time, was rescued at the end of the fifties by the incendiary nihilists led by his compatriot González Arango.

For my father's generation, the maestro who wrote *Otraparte* was their precursor, for he reflects with great simplicity upon the usual themes that he immediately demolishes with irony, or he pokes fun at Colombians, expressing their convictions and fears; he admires young bodies in bed, he laments the faces of old age in others, he recounts his love for the earth and the sky on the foothills of the Volcano del Ruiz, which he climbs to observe Manizales, a city already changed by the coffee boom and filled with concrete, something rather unfamiliar in 1928. He was an observer, a traveler in the most lovable meaning of the word. The incredible thing is that he travels by foot and people find it strange he doesn't have a mule. On his trip he is considered a madman, a crazy wanderer. And nowadays to want to see a bit more of a place while on assignment is qualified as romantic, illusionary, useless, eccentric.

Getting used to a new unknown city helps me recuperate the emotion of travel. When I stay in a place months without going anywhere a frightening desperation fills me, I can't breathe well at night, no place pleases me, I feel like breaking into rage or passing out. At the same time, I used to have long lapses between trips back home, but in April I went to the International Book Fair in Bogotá and returned in October for the Eje Cafetero Book Fair in my beloved Manizales, which with tremendous generosity decorated me October 14 as a Knight of the Order. Vargas Vila used to criticize Amado Nervo for bowing and scraping to get decorations, but in this case I let myself kneel with pleasure because it was a concession awarded by my hometown.

The other trip was to New York, where just a few days after the occasion in Manizales I presented the English edition of my novel *Boulevard of Heroes,* a work that originally took nine years of writing. It had a theme that seemed *demodé*: the delirium of a crazy Latin American guerilla in Paris and the Bolivarian jungles of the Orinoco. It was held at the America's Society on Park Avenue with the presence of the mythic Gregory Rabassa, the man whose generosity and assistance made possible the publication. As Simón Bolívar would say, "Now I can be peacefully lowered into my grave" with a prologue written by Rabassa, whom we Colombians consider a bit more than a god of language for his excellent translation of Gabriel García Márquez's *One Hundred years of Solitude* and *In Evil Hour*, along with a dozen other works, including Julio Cortázar's *Hopscotch* and several novels by other Latin American writers. Rabassa posits in that introduction that such a theme as insurrection or dictatorship isn't a unique monopoly of the regionalists or members of the boom, for it is recurrent in Hispano-American literature inscribed within the wave of the Cervantine novel. Isn't *Don Quixote* a novel about insurrection?

Such diverse emotions joined together this year outside Mexico City have generated a terrible anxiety, a crazy desire to leave Mexico and go live somewhere else: in New York, definitely *the* city above all others, or in my coffee-growing lands on the slopes of a volcano, reflecting upon the world while I lounge in a hammock, or in the cold rainy air of Bogotá in an old house filled with furniture smelling of freshly carded wool and damp wood, discussing literature with friends next to a roaring fireplace.

Voyages, passing through airports, the time spent on flights, the new aromas and atmospheres of each place excite and awake the traveler's monster, that terrible minotaur which bellowing ceaselessly begins to wander through the labyrinth. I once took a trip for ten days to Puerto Vallarta, staying at the city's best hotel in one of its nicest rooms facing the ocean, surrounded by hundreds of ecologists and government officials there to discuss the fate of whales throughout the world. To spend so many days immersed in the theme of whales made me feel like a contemporary Jonah.

To travel opens the wounds of memories of other cities — Stockholm discovered in its May luminosity; Berlin in its snowy February chill that possesses its own unmistakable aroma; London in December; Rome in January, icy cold, dark, delicious; Barcelona in spring with the flower-filled Ramblas; Los Angeles in December, hanging out at the beach in a Studebaker; Mexico City during the September rains accompanied by a beautiful young woman of some still living pre-Hispanic race, with bright white teeth and tawny skin and deep black hair; Paris lustrous in April, on the banks of the Seine or before the Grand Palais or Invalides. Unique, unforgettable days, each one equal to a hundred or a thousand days of nauseating routine. And when the traveler comes back to a city a second time, he wanders down those now known and intimate streets, recognizing the smells and colors, the winding lanes, the unique and secret nooks and crannies; he surrenders to the sorrow of friends who have changed or disappeared, who no longer go to the same bars or live on the same streets where they experienced happy and bitter scenes. Two travelers equally lost, one just barely in the first trance of the initiate, the other dedicated to taking a look at things with a certain dose of wisdom.

The status of traveler and foreigner, along with lover, are the only ones which you can live in a flash of lightening. Arriving to a new city is like approaching an unknown body: your senses are in a total state of alert. Manhattan smells like the woman you've always desired and searched for who is at last beside you, caressing your face with her hands; she lets you feel her breath, she brings you ships just anchored in port. Each time I return to New York it feels like the astute and adored woman who re-creates us as she makes us her own. Bogotá is like that, too, another special lover that each time I visit takes me with her nocturnal wind, her damp futuristic streets, her bars and special pleasures. And she is my lover, too, that horrible Mexico City, which like every great lover is hated and loved at the same time, the whore city, the assassin city, the vaporous city. Stockholm, a sister of oceanic water and bridges and bends, foggy hills, salty wharves, barefoot women in flowery cotton robes with long hair smelling of the essence of a Nordic forest. No city can be forgotten. Their aroma, their voice, their eyes, the scratches from their fingernails, the shriek of their depths, the texture of their tapestries, their perfumes, the way they disappear on street corners, all figures projected in an unending film. Ibagué in adolescence, Cali and Cartago in childhood, Victoria, La Dorada, Tegucigalpa, Guatemala City, Tapachula, Coatzacoalcos, Zacatecas, Bordeaux, Toulouse, Nancy, Tours, Panama City, Managua, San Francisco, San José, Cartagena de Indias, Barranquilla, Riohacha, all of them women I've loved. I will end this year of travel in San Cristóbal de las Casas, still on that circumnavigation I've been experiencing for decades, but immersed in the other definitive voyage, the inexplicable, miraculous voyage of life. What does this city possess that it convokes such dreams, makes them flower as if out of a sacred lamp holding a marvelous genie?

Saturday, December 24

I LIVED IN Paris almost six years, between April 1974 and December 1979. I arrived in spring, and after putting my suitcases in a locker at Orly Airport I took the metro, got out at Invalides and strolled along the banks of the Seine, looking at the cupolas of the Grand Palais with *Le Nouvel Observateur* under my arm. I studied political economy with a minor in philosophy at the crazy University of Vincennes-Paris VIII, located in a forest of the same name and created to lodge the madhouse of May '68. There is a worldwide brotherhood of the children of that campus — Arabs, Africans, South Americans — that happily carry the denomination of *Vincennois*. There were the movements of women's liberation and Third Worldism, exiles from Latin America who had been wounded and embittered by dictatorship. I was touched by the Vietnam War, the death of Mao, the government of Giscard d'Estaing, the apotheosis of Barthes, Foucault, Deleuze and Guattari, Schérer and Chatelet, the sad twilight of Sartre and Simone de Beauvoir, the last acts of the cells of the ultra-left, delicious years of freedom and demonstrations.

Everything was a kind of dream, during the Cold War but before the sinister resurgence of xenophobia.

Brezshnev in power. The fall of Nixon. The first films of Isabelle Adjani, whom I once saw in a phone booth on the Boulevard Saint Michel making a movie. The huge demonstration after the assassination of Pierre Goldman, the *gauchiste* author of *Souvenirs obscurs d'un juif polonais né en France (The Obscure Memories of a Polish Jew Born in France).* Sunday afternoons, the music of Frehel and Damia, one night at the cinema in Trocadero when we asked for our money back from the legendary Henri Langlois in protest of a lousy movie. Trips to Rome, Barcelona, Berlin, Frankfurt, Copenhagen, Stockholm, London. Reading Cortázar while laying next to a beautiful woman, reading Borges on the metro, reading insatiably Stendhal, Balzac and Flaubert in the subterranean dens of Belleville. Preventive visits to the Hospital Saint Louis to cure small bouts of venereal disease and running into friends there, all of us avid practitioners before the sinister appearance of AIDS. The world of Sunday markets in summer months with friends or luminous lovers when we prepared our long feasts of food and drink. Nights at Chez Georges and other places in St. Germain. Brazilian dances at Wagram Hall. Concerts by Lluis Llach, Julien Clerc, Véronique Samson, Georges Moustaki, Maxime Leforestier, Mercedes Sosa and Joan Manuel Serrat. In the end crazy unforgettable years from some movie that come back to me fifteen years later in San Cristóbal de las Casas.

I eat breakfast and read the papers at the Hotel Santa Clara. Three colorful old *papagayos* are out of their cage, free a little while in the sun. I like to take refuge in this place where there are no customers. At the Casa Vieja, where there's nothing really to write about, a few young journalists strut about as if they were guarding a great secret. I flee and take my place near the Cathedral with some books, this notebook, and my cell phone.

After years of agitation in the great urb, Mexico City,

where even the most lucid person loses perspective of life in the middle of the smog and stress (such modern words), I used to not take pleasure in such peace. Millions of cars driving down thousands and thousands of avenues, expelling the exhaust of progress. At noon people choke on the smell of burning things and everybody goes around in his vehicle and gets stuck in traffic for hours, yet people hang onto the feeling of power that a car lends. But who invented this madness? Do its victims know that the automobile god dismembers cities and destroys parks in order to construct avenues, intersections, freeways? I belong to that strange fraternity of people who never learned to drive and when we tried were unable. Now we make virtue out of necessity, but I think we're right. This path was wrong. Like all chimeras of this absurd progress, that of an auto for each person managed to triumph not out of necessity but in order to feed the earnings of all-powerful capital. To breathe real air, without the metropolitan chaos, seems a miracle. Nothing is going on at the church, the cell phone is silent. The papagayos screech while I drink my coffee. It's been a long time since I saw a papagayo.

Later I go to a peace demonstration consisting of about a hundred people, maybe twenty Indians and the rest young tourists and photographers. At the front they carry on placards the image of the Virgin of Guadalupe, while a mariachi group plays a song in their honor. We pass down the street by La Quimera Bookstore and I decide to break off and enter to look around. The peace march is rather sparsely attended, but the journalists will take it upon themselves to blow it up. I've already said it, this event has been inflated out of the needs of the world press. As there appears to be no news anywhere in the world, maybe just a civil war in Chechnya or some highjacking or tidal wave, at this end of the year something must be made out of the

Zapatistas. On the outside they will think San Cristóbal is under siege, that women are crying in the basements worried that war and bombings are about to begin. What's going on is total indifference, everyone in a hurry to buy gifts and ingredients for their Christmas dinner. The daily newspapers will have people demonstrating for peace, when the march is mostly made up of tourists and photographers: it is a masturbatory demonstration for the journalists from the mass media, desperate to send something to justify their expense accounts and per diems. The people are demonstrating, but in the markets and stores. It's like the bishop's fast. He would like to be a new Gandhi, but he has very few followers, except for a few blessed people and the journalists who come by in the afternoon to listen to him. Of course, outside they will think there are hordes fasting for peace, that the masses flood the church in support of the prelate. That isn't true at all. The journalistic machine unceasingly inflates and inflates, falsifies and falsifies this bulletless paper war.

In the afternoon, after a cynical and severe vice minister gives a press conference at the rectory to announce that contacts with the Zapatistas regarding a peace dialogue were advancing, I go eat with Omar, a photographer from the daily *Reforma*, and Oswaldo Jiménez at the restaurant El Teatro. They have good food and an intimate atmosphere, candle-lit tables, quick service and a view of the ochre-tiled roofs of the city. The conversation is intense, including of course current events in Chiapas, and concludes with mystical themes, reflections on death, the nature of art and photography, and the possible reconciliation of the languages of the photographer and the writer.

I've written since I've been twelve. At fifteen my idols were Verne, Wilde, Whitman, Lorca, Kafka, Dostoievsky and José Asunción Silva. Since then I haven't stopped for a moment. Even during periods when I don't write, I remain an absolute writer, and will stay one to the grave. I love seeing how time authorizes perspectives, how words become a friendlier terrain: one swims in their labyrinths, one calls them forth not only for their meaning but for their sound. They are sound and material, they open doors and close them, they are keys to strange worlds and platforms to distant or interior planets.

This night the Casa Vieja holds a dinner for journalists far from home, forced to be in San Cristóbal and sit at tables set with place cards. With us is the cameraman Carrillo, a really funny Mexican guy who possesses a clear and fresh perspective. Oswaldo is an American of Ecuadorian origin who relates to us the difficult experiences of growing up "Hispanic" in the United States. He's a sensible guy, also one of the few people here these days who looks beyond his camera or notebook. There's also a really nice fellow, a reporter from *El Mundo* in Madrid. I have no idea why but before the dinner begins, while having a drink at the table in the courtyard, I'm assaulted by the memory of a some texts by the great lovers of women, Casanova and Sade among the eighteenth century libertines and Klaus Kinski and Roger Vadim among our contemporaries.

The eighteenth-century libertine was as lucid and cynical as that of today. Perhaps back then there was more danger in the search for sex, because of moral reasons, although its commerce was more intense then than now because of the leisure of those years, together with the open air of the forests and the darkness and abundance of stables and granaries. For today's libertine the city can be an impediment: time, distance, the cost of hotels, police in the parks, can put off his designs.

Vadim wrote, it seems out of need for money, the story of his affairs with three beautiful women from our time, Brigitte Bardot, Catherine Deneuve and Jane Fonda, as well as other women even more beautiful but less famous. His prose establishes links with the eighteenth-century libertines and their resplendent gynophilia: the libertine is the greatest friend of woman, the least macho, at heart the most tender and fragile, the madonna's greatest accomplice. Kinski, a notably febrile version of the satyr, speaks of his incessant search. Wherever he goes, from one side of the planet to another, he recounts to us his seduction of camerawomen, nurses, cooks, actresses, screenwriters or in his worst moments visits to whorehouses seeking the unexpected rewards of fat Pakistani prostitutes.

Women will agree that without satyrs and Casanovas the world would be a sad desert. These specimens of men are always available and the scent of a woman will take them anywhere; but most importantly they depart and leave behind nothing more than the trace of happiness, of kisses, excitement, penetration. While others live in the numbing world of matrimony, with its stupid fidelities and guilt, the Casanova has his way and disappears at dawn before the world takes notice, like a movie cowboy, a solitary man who undertakes his retreat on the endless avenues of night, leaving the pleasant memory of his aroma.

This Christmas evening let us pray for the souls of satyrs, let us kneel and ask eternal peace for Casanovas and lovers, let us implore the Lord for the souls of Giacomo Casanova, Klaus Kinski, Roger Vadim, Restif de Bretonne, the Guillaume Apollinaire of *Les onze mille verges,* for the glory of Rodolphe, the great betraying lover of Madame Bovary, let us pray for the flowering incense of pre-Hispanic *Chacmols* filled with copal and invoke the playful spirits of every libertine from history and literature, as wise and linked to divinity as are poets.

The conversation at table, accompanied by the delicious beers brewed for Christmas and sickening sweet pastries, takes a natural turn toward what every encounter of bored and tired journalists or travelers on Christmas Eve leads to, when suddenly around midnight sporadic dusty bursts are heard coming from the street, the first thing close to gunfire we've heard in the five days of coming and going. At this time of the night, other more fortunate journalists will be practicing in reality the theories of Klaus Kinski or Roger Vadim, but those here tonight are pitiful and looking pretty homely: no woman has swooned and fallen at their feet, or they've already fallen asleep dreaming of heading into Zapatista territory at dawn; the only woman this evening, a young doctor with a kind of strange contorted face, but still sort of interesting, is surrounded by big-bellied men who stand in line to dance with her, and when she twirls on the dance floor her skirt spins to reveal long splendid legs.

Fatigue conquers everyone in their state of failed reporters, absent from the Christmas rituals of family. I try to lift my spirits with a double espresso. The holiday period makes me think of some books I'd like to read, *The Tomb Without Tranquility* by Cyril Conolly, suggested by a young Mexican writer Adolfo Castañon; *The Breviary of Rot* by E. Cioran, who says that "tout mot est un mal de plus," every word is another evil; or a book the poet and essayist Vicente Quirarte lent me whose old pages and solid leather cover come to memory, *La contraguérrilla française au Mexique: Souvenirs des terres chaudes,* by the crazy general Kératry.

But my greatest desire is sleep. We're all tired. It's a perfect atmosphere for useless drunken discussions. The party is petering out. The waiters clean away the tables gracefully arranged for the Mexican and foreign correspondents, forced to be there tonight by the Zapatistas and the Mexican army.

I go out into the street and walk to the Zócalo. San Cristóbal at three in the morning is enchanting in its cold damp and penetrating cold. Cast by the street lamps, my shadow moves in a serpentine grace. A drunk vomits on the corner. A taxi takes me back to the house and I fall like a rock into a deep sleep.

In my dreams I hear the cry "Viva Zapata" and the sound of machine guns.

Sunday, December 25

AN ABSURD DAY, Sunday, and moreover December 25, something truly frightening. The city is deserted and even the sun seems tired. History has stopped and in the afternoon I have nothing left to do but go to the Cathedral where the bishop fasts along with several blessed women and the saintly dark young woman. From coming here so often I've become accustomed to the chapel where the bishop reads, prays and receives the visits of Indians, at present Chamulas who recite strange litanies while the cold intensifies with the oncoming night. They pass around prayer sheets they read enthusiastically. The canticles and litanies become louder until they create an increasingly hysterical spectacle coordinated by a fanatical fat pale woman in round eyeglasses. I take refuge on one of the dark wooden pews and pass peacefully through the undertow from last night's drinks. Among the blessed women I seem like another middle-class foreigner, and I flee when the fanatical woman suddenly comes toward me ready to make me read a prayer.

I like this cold and the icy wind passing through the naves, penetrating through the immense portals which make me remember my childhood near the Volcán del Ruiz. I'm a little heliophobic: I love to bundle up in coats and scarves and enter cozy places to have a glass of hot wine. I am, well, tonight, a *coleto* from the cold land, as they call themselves here those of the real or fictitious white race, those descendents of the Spaniards who wore a leather jacket known as a *coleto* and inhabited the manorial city during the colonial era. The "authentic" *coletos* hate Ruiz and demonstrate against the Zapatistas and even insult Amado Avendaño, the governor "in rebellion" of Chiapas, for being from Soconusco, that is, for being an outlander from the coast.

During the colonial era Chiapas was divided by the Spaniards into various regions named Llanos, Zoques, Quelenes, Zendales, Soconusco and Chiapa, these last terms no doubt coming from the Nahua words *xoconochco* and *chiapan*, according to the historian Jean de Vos. Centuries later those strange names resound again in this pre-Hispanic colonial night. The wind runs through the streets and carries in its material the afternoon prayers. I make out the eyes of old Indians on this starry night, eyes of silence, eyes of light, eyes a thousand years old, eyes joined to the earth. Church bells centuries old ring at the exact hour marked by the clepsydras, the same sounds that echoed throughout the mountains and paths of other times. Everything here has a pre-Hispanic energy: the Indians don't want to be white and are less than interested in that world. They turn their backs on progress, on modernity; they want to live in the circular time they perceive in the lands surrounding the former convent and church of Santo Domingo where they gather to sell their handicrafts to tourists. But the *coletos* also turn their back on progress, anchored to their old racism and their old manias of last names and families nostalgic for some ridiculous aristocracy.

1994 was a year full of surprises in Mexico with unexpected guerrillas, assassinations of politicians and future presidents, and a few slow changes in the country's dismal political inertia. The silence here this twenty-fifth of December brings me near a centuries-old peace, but where everything used to transpire anchored in differences: the submissive Indian, the arrogant white on the rump of a horse, *de coleta* the proud *coleto.*

On our continent, as everywhere in the world, racism is common currency: the whites hate the blacks and vice-versa, the Indians hate the blacks, the whites scorn the Indians and the latter don't trust the former. The Mexican Revolution broke with ancestral vices still at work in other countries and it's true that an important percentage of *mestizos,* mixed-blood people, have risen in social position to important posts and that in the capital among certain milieus such discrimination isn't quite so notorious. Despite everything, thousands and thousands of building rooftops in the capital are the somnambulistic city of immigrant Indians who work for miserable wages as the servants of poor whites, poor mestizos and poor Indians who try to forget their origin.

But in the interior of the country the question gets more complicated, reaching its extreme in the hinterlands of Chiapas. And so it goes along the length and breadth of the continent, varying in tone and intensity. We're here close to Guatemala and you feel it. We should be aware that this land declared its fidelity to the Mexican federation rather late in time and could have been a separate country like El Salvador, Honduras, Guatemala — fractions of the great pre-Hispanic world of the Mayan orbit, Balkanized ever after. Sometimes one feels this is no longer Mexico but a generic kind of Latin America, far from the rituals of the Mexican high plains. While the Europeans and Anglo-Saxons wandering down these streets are fascinated by this mysterious world, we Latin Americans touch here the truth of our strange and complex mixture.

Once at a conference at the Palace of Fine Arts in Mexico City, before he died of cancer, the Uruguayan critic Emir Rodríguez Monegal said that as a student in England, he began to believe himself a kind of Brit and one day he understood, perhaps too late, he was just some gaucho from the pampas whose culture began in the southern region of the United States and extended all the way to Patagonia. And what happened to Rodríguez Monegal is as pathetic as the pretension of so many Europeans who in good faith believe themselves to be ex-Frenchmen or ex-Germans converted into Mexicans, Caribbeans or South Americans. But everywhere throughout the Americas, and the world, at this turn of the millenium, differences have been stirred up and the children of immigrants give the dark eye to today's stonily silent guests. Consider all the national, ethnic and religious conflicts which have spilled blood that erupted in the years since the fall of the Berlin Wall in 1989 and the dissolution of the Soviet Union. Chiapas is another soft ethnic war, not of course Mexico's first bitter dose.

A key book in understanding the current conflict is *Zapata and the Mexican Revolution*, by John Womack, Jr. The author presents the actions almost a century ago of the original Zapatistas who inspired those of today. In that distant 1909, in Anenecuilco, Morelos, near the capital, the already worn out old nobles of the town passed the baton to a youthful thirty-year-old man who became one of the century's heroes, an emblem of Mexicanicity, alive more now than ever. Just as has taken place in Chiapas over the last decade, that first peasant rebellion was due to the arrogant technocrats of the period, the so-called *scientifics* who didn't understand the needs of those people who had turned their back on the cosmopolitan idea of progress in order to conserve their customs and centuries-old tranquility. Just as now, the center wanted to impose some little *señor* named Escandón, a graduate of London schools; it gave priority to ranchers over peasants and played upon the latter's supposed ancestral submissiveness to remove them by force from their lands. Then as now the rebellion against the center didn't take long, and, after the fall of the dictator Díaz, the rulers of the country were forced to negotiate. A decade later, one April 10, Zapata was betrayed and machine-gunned to death at a hacienda in Chinameca. Here, it seems, the clumsiness of the new *científicos* will perhaps conclude with another bloody episode and tragedy will give birth to another emblematic figure.

Zapata died at thirty-nine and Marcos must be about that old now. Rebellions are a matter of youth. Old people no longer have any strength but the edict of their corruption. I look at the photos in Womack's beautiful book: Zapata in 1909, in a hat and ranch clothes astride a beautiful sorrel, with the hard look of a *caudillo,* a political strongman; Zapata and his Zapatista bodyguards of that era, with cartridge belts and wooden rifles like those of today; Zapata beside the democratic and spiritualist president Madero in Cuautla; in the presidential chair next to Pancho Villa in 1914; at the table next to President Eulalio Gutiérrez, José Vasconcelos and Pancho Villa at the luncheon in the Palacio Nacional; Zapatistas eating breakfast at the Sanborn's on Madero, where I have eaten so many times myself before going to my office at the Latin American Tower; and, finally, Zapata dead, swollen, machine-gunned, his crying devoted followers beside him.

This is the spinning wheel of history, a circular repetition that demonstrates in its capriciousness the vanity of linear progress. That past episode occurred in the state of Morelos, one of the first lands conquered by Cortés and the other conquistadors and Maximiliano's viceregal seat; at this moment history repeats itself in distant Chiapas near old convents and churches. With that great ability of the studious Americans, Womack analyzes the causes of the Zapatista revolution that might be applied with some shadings to the current situation, describing a group of politicians, the so-called *científicos,* who believed themselves infallible and were certain that Mexico could only succeed through their control and authority. From the 1890s to the first decade of the 1900s, they lectured the nation with a sense of entitlement, but by 1908, with their maneuvering exposed, "the powerful proved naïve, treacherous, and incompetent. In a short time their fashionable order collapsed."

Perhaps I should recall that those oppositions are alive in the rest of the continent. *Cholos* and mountain dwellers in Peru, Colombian immigrants and people from the hinterlands in Venezuela; *cachacos, corronchos,* Indians, blue-eyed whites and blacks in Colombia, Indians and whites in Guatemala: a never-ending history. *Civilization and Barbarie* by Sarmiento, *Ariel and Caliban* by the Uruguayan José Enrique Rodó, Indians exploited by gum tappers in the Amazon, as the Colombian José Eustasio Rivera describes in *The Whirlpool* and as well Ricardo Güiraldes in *Don Segundo Sombra, Yawar Fiesta* by José Maria Arguedas, *Men of Corn* by Miguel Ángel Asturias, *Doña Barbara* by Romulo Gallegos, an interminable list of grievances and searches within young nations that are barely two centuries old.

My generation opened its eyes to literature and ideas in a turbulent adolescence at the end of the '60s and the beginning of the '70s, when Latin America became once again the prisoner of another nationalist and messianic episode, but at the same time left behind its marginality. I turned fifteen in 1968, when out of France surged a rebellion key for later modes of thought. That same year the death in Bolivia of Ernesto *Che* Guevara still resonated, and as well the not so distant fall in battle of the Colombian guerrilla priest Camilo Torres, and the peace-and-love culture in the United States that exploded with all its force amidst a counterculture rebelling against the war in Vietnam and racism. I remember that year the death of Martin Luther King, the heart transplant operation on Philip Blaiberg in South Africa at the hands of the charismatic Dr. Barnard, a kind of mythological Dr. Kildare from the old American television drama. The biggest rock stars were performing, we Colombians had just discovered Gabriel García Márquez's *One Hundred Years of Solitude* and to our libraries came the books of Carlos Fuentes and Juan Rulfo, from Paris those of the Argentine Julio Cortázar, from Spain those of the Peruvian Mario Vargas Llosa, from Cuba those of Guillermo Cabrera Infantes, from Buenos Aires those of Jorge Luis Borges. Latin America lived at that moment beneath the messianic mantle of the Cuban Revolution and youths across the entire continent wished to enlist, with the final disgrace being that many evolved not on the libertarian side of the rebels of '68 Paris or the psychedelic pacifists from San Francisco, but on the most homicidal and sectarian paths of Maoism, pro-Soviet Stalinism and the cult of Castro. Before them opened the Pandora's box of strong militaristic tendencies utilizing genocidal methods of repression.

That year in Manizales we welcomed the visit of Pablo Neruda in the apotheosis of his glory, just a few years after he won the Nobel Prize. Something extraordinary occurred at his reading at the Teatro Fundadores: thousands of people young and old packed the auditorium until the glass doors shattered and the crowd surged all the way up to the stage where the old man read his work aloud in his nasal voice, sitting beside his last wife, Matilde Urrutia. Neruda, who had already disavowed his wonderful poems from *Residence on Earth* for not being exemplary and optimistic enough for youth, sang of landscapes and volcanoes and through his poetry we confronted "Yankee imperialism," which just barely a year before had put the first man on the moon, while he sang of the goodness of the Bolshevik revolution. At fifteen that literary and political excitement inundated our brains and in cafés we entered into a fratricidal struggle between pro-Soviets, Maoists, Trotskyites, Castristas.

At school we poets began to be looked at with suspicion and one night, in front of the Cathedral, a "revisionist" Maoist of that time, now serving time in a French prison for drug-trafficking, threatened me with a knife for being a "petit bourgeois" who couldn't choose between poetry and revolution. Another guy got furious at me because I gave in to the temptation of trading fifty copies of the magazine *Peking Report* for an Aguilar edition of *The Iliad*. In the Colombian mountains, the pro-Castro guerrillas shot their companions for having betrayed the revolution by not accepting their dogma. From the northern mountains came the proclamations of the Popular Army of Liberation with their motto "Eternal glory to comrade Pedro Vázquez Rendón" and mimeographed editions of Stalin and Lenin were passed around clandestinely like Biblical texts. From Cuba they had told us "Revolution or Death" and a sinister Latin Americanist rhetoric was already percolating about the famous "compromised" literature. Jorge Luis Borges began to be the intelligent tempting demon many read in secret. The great stars of the boom were on the side of Fidel Castro, converted into the grand commander of the continent's liberation: "Everything within the revolution, nothing outside it." Revolutionary songs were sung in the glow of campfires. That melody still resounds — "Rise up, rise up, the world is ours" — chanted by enthusiastic adolescents.

Looking at those years from the perspective of this turn of the century, I would say they're similar to the conspiratorial atmospheres described by Dostoievsky and other Russian authors at the end of the nineteenth century, and later by Joseph Conrad in that beautiful book, *Under Western Eyes*. Latin American youth felt themselves characters in some novel about a conspiracy during the time of the czars: clandestinity, spies, secret police, suicidal people ready to offer their lives for the revolution, and jails filled with tortured rebels. In the following years more episodes would add to the escalade. In Chile arrived Salvador Allende and in Colombia at the National University we later all felt deep sorrow at the coup d'état and Augusto Pinochet's ascendance behind his dark, traitorous glasses. Chained to the radio we waited for the reaction of General Pratts and the retaking of Santiago by the proletarians, not knowing that on that eleventh of September, 1973, we were attending the funeral of a dream.

Afterwards the exodus from South America to Europe would take place. Reaching Paris in 1974 saved me from the darkness reigning in Colombia and Latin America in general: at its universities the dominion of sects, and, on the other side, the dirty wars of governments with hundreds of disappeared from every faction. In the "exile" of Paris we lived a comfortable nostalgia and in that secondary capital of Latin America we discovered our otherness. But the Europeans still embraced us in solidarity, recounting to us by heart the stories of Aureliano Buendía and Remedios the Beauty, and many of them remembered the not so distant war of the Holocaust with its persecution and death. It was wonderful to be a Latin American in Europe during those years in the womb of ideas which later spread throughout this continent. *The Anti-Oedipus* by Deleuze and Guattari, *The Order of Things* by Foucault, *Of*

Grammatology by Jacques Derrida, the works of Althusser, Greimas, the old and drooling Sartre, the "new philosophy," Roland Barthes and semiology, the Third Worldism of Gunder Frank and Samir Amim, but as well the cinema of Pasolini and the lustrous sculptures of César.

The years have gone by, we have survived the period of Thatcher and Reagan, the dream of the self-regulating free market seems another ideology that hopefully will someday crumble and fall. So it's nothing strange this neo-hippyism of San Cristóbal, the eagerness of today's twenty-year-olds for a new cause, this time indigenous people and their white leader Marcos, the atypical guerrilla, a reader of Foucault and Althusser, a lover of classical and Latin American literature. A post-'68 child barely forty with a lively writing style, at times a bit cloying but other times effective.

Once again the world is upside down and satellites pass through the tropical sky. This is Latin America: Bolívar and Santa Anna, Rosas and Sarmiento, the gaucho and the immigrant, the knife-wielder and the little priss, losers and university graduates, Emiliano Zapata and José Vasconcelos, Jorge Amado and the concrete poets, Vinicius de Moraes and the *cumbia,* Mexican pop singer Juan Gabriel and Argentine governor Palito Ortega, the tango and Spanish rock. Potosí and Maracaibo, La Paz and Barranquilla, Monterrey and Zacatecas, Havana and Valparaíso, the Bay of San Salvador and Puebla, Buenos Aires and Iquitos, Manaos and Miami, Salvador Allende and Pinochet, Pablo Neruda and Pablo de Rokha. A Latin America that like a guru attracts Europeans and Americans, because this is the Far West, the strange cocktail of the Enlightenment and colorful exotic fruits and exuberant foliage, overwhelming creativity and exciting bodies, chaos and pleasure, flesh and intelligence, fakery and splendor.

Monday, December 26

SAN CRISTÓBAL de las Casas has returned to normal. From the capital arrive senators and politicians of diverse stripes who hope to prevent the exchange of accusations and the outbreak of confrontation. The meetings are held at the parish house, while at the seat of the provisional government in rebellion gather volunteers who wish to go to Guadalupe Tepeyac with provisions for the rebel troops and demand that the military checkpoints stop impeding their passage. In San Andrés Larráinzar new rebel trenches appear. Journalists of different nationalities try to meet Zapatistas at any cost and travel by diverse routes. At the end of the afternoon some come back deceived, others happy because they were able to find the masked ones.

At last the daily newspapers arrive. A splendid sun reigns throughout the day. Prices rise in the stores while the country sinks into a financial crisis reminiscent of 1982. Foreigners don't take much notice of the multiplication of their dollars into pesos. For me this is normal. Since childhood I have heard of devaluation, inflation, scarcity, the fall of ministers, troubled presidents: all part of the folklore from throughout the Americas. Capital lite, corruption, modern ideologies falling into decay, yesterday the boys from Chicago, today those from Harvard and Yale. The gurus used to be Milton Friedman, Margaret Thatcher and Fukuyama. Decades ago Keynes and Galbraith. Kennedy's Alliance for Progress. Reaganomics. Bush and Clinton's Free Trade Agreement. The New Deal. The Monroe Doctrine. The Peace Corps. Protectionism, state interventionism, economic planning, free markets. Open borders. Coups d'état, elections, protests. The interminable fair of man's great ideas. They used to say with certainty that men pass and ideas remain; now we must say that ideas pass and man remains.

In Colombia, like all over the world, people love to discuss politics and everything revolves around those slippery characters from political parties and soccer teams. The archetypal newspaper, whether national or regional — almost the only spiritual nourishment for most Colombians, and what consolidates the country's sad culture — has virtually stayed the same for decades. The same columnists, but now the sons or grandsons of the old-timers, write long solemn paragraphs about local political gossip, where like in some soap opera the branches of the same families from a half-century ago are implicated. Seldom do you see in their pages a lucid article by a political scientist or a historian, only babbling texts that would shame the pages of any provincial newspaper in every other country on the continent.

When I was a child I used to go with my father to those cafés where affectionate old men talked about politics and commented on those innocuous articles in the dailies as no doubt their grandchildren will someday. In a similar way radio contributes to the idolatry of academics and every move by this diseased caste is described step by step to a population ever more stupefied by the mass media. When as a child during the '60s I went with my father to Bogotá, I used to listen to those commentaries about the future of the country, shortages, currency devaluations and, something more emotional, the actions of some guerilla movement, the death of a hero or a riot among the population caused by inflation.

I have the clearest memory: we were passing by the Plaza de Bolívar, in front of the Capitol, one midmorning on a cold and luminous day. My father and his friends were engaged in conversation as we walked down 11th Street toward Avenida Jiménez. My father entered for a moment the Banco Industrial Colombiano, where he had his account, and then came out smiling. We emerged in front of the government office building and the legendary Buchholz Bookstore, and went into a café, perhaps El Pasaje or the St. Moritz.There those old men's incessant conversation continued about the destinies of politicians, a speech by some Liberal or Conservative, in the end the interminable history heard in South American cafés that made those penetrating men in fedoras, three-piece suits, starched shirts and dark ties, occasionally carrying an umbrella, so content to discuss. Bogotá from the first half of the century lives there, like in the novels of José Antonio Osorio Lizarazo: men reading the newspapers *El Tiempo* and *El Spectador* at the St. Moritz, people playing billiards in the background, guys who got you to buy their drinks for them, drunks and tipplers, *aguardiente,* vendors of lottery tickets, shoe shiners, the street life of the first decade of the National Front's pact between Liberals and Conservatives, signed to give the illusion that the violence which erupted after the death of Jorge Eliécer Gaitán just a few blocks from there — April 9, 1948, a date etched in the mind of Colombians — was behind us.

The system has always maintained itself and the same grand political families continue to dominate, the same clever ones monopolize the seats of power and sinecures. Nothing has changed and nothing will change. At this time of night it all makes me laugh, like all the ink spilled in Mexico about the coming changes that, sometimes I dare think, aren't even desired by the ones searching for them.

Octavio Paz, the polemical Mexican guru and offspring of an Andalusian mother, a *Porfirista* grandfather, and a father who was an activist in the old *Zapatismo*, speaks of our Hispanic-Arabic tradition and in many of his writings he penetrates into the defects of continental identity: bureaucracy, rhetoric, discourse, corruption, nepotism, cruelty, bigotry, *caudillismo,* strongman rule — the vices from which neither opposition members nor government officials are exempt. In his already classic book *The Labyrinth of Solitude,* written some four decades ago, and in other later works, Paz passionately investigates the underlying characteristics of Mexicanicity. One can agree or disagree with his conclusions, but his effort to understand his nation's origins and destiny, looking at recent, colonial or pre-Hispanic historical episodes while writing about its literature and art, is a laudable example for the rest of the Americas. His existence is key to contemporary Mexico and hopefully Latin America can count on people like him, that is, willing to think and be wrong, of course, and not just write journalistic chronicles that reproduce the usual assumptions, sheeplike discourse that supplicates public opinion or those in power and always fears to take the bull by the horns.

Throughout my many years in Mexico, the texts of Paz have provided me a light in which to try and understand this country: its local and external roots, its masks and sorrows, its scars and doubts, its rituals and lies, its pyramids and silences, its cruelty and courtesy. I've also been irritated by his severe tone in addressing those on the left who struggle against power and his ever greater tolerance for the regime and its money hawks. But I've had him here beside me these last days. I've reread *Ladera este*, an excellent collection of poems, and I try to understand how the Zapatistas whipped up public opinion.

I was saying how the opposition and those in power in Latin America are sometimes two sides of the same coin. On this continent members of the opposition wait to obtain a quota of power so they can repeat the same vices: the Colombian guerillas turned into businessmen; after the holocaust in El Salvador, the former guerrilla leaders were happy to take over the clubs and mansions of those they fought against. And even more, they wish to be the new oligarchs. When they take union or political power, Argentine, Peruvian, Chilean, Mexican or Nicaraguan opposition members have fallen into the same plagued defects of patronage, ghost positions from which they derive salaries without working, embezzlement, jewels on their fingers, gold watches, silver teeth, private whorehouses run by the public treasury, tons of mansions illicitly obtained.

The aspiration of converting this continent into a society under the rule of law, where talent and merit are rewarded and not wit and intrigue, is more than utopian. From Mexico, definitely a special case in the context of Latin America due to its complexity and richness, passing through the small Central American republics to the Caribbean and Andean nations all the way to Patagonia, such a dream of legality is a chimera. The clever and cynical have the game won before it's even started, those with integrity and good faith rest beneath the ground. The clowns take power; the statesmen with integrity, if they exist, are ostracized; such is the great truism of Latin American politics.

On this day of clean air the newspapers report, as is *de rigeur,* Mexico's economic bankruptcy and people frightened by the magnitude of the devaluation of the currency, the scarcity of reserves, capital flight, possible conditions for international loans and the reaction of the all-powerful neighbor, the United States. The clever investors who move their money around saved themselves a short while back and the population which voted in mass for continuity in 1994 will still pay out of their pocketbook for what was sacked by those laudable impresarios, those "generators of jobs who are well-paid because they are so necessary," as the unimaginative speeches of technocrats always state. The same story from 1982 is repeated, when the country fell into bankruptcy after years of dream and dissipation generated by the delirium of oil; the same history as Venezuela and Brazil and every nation of this continent Balkanized into fiefdoms ruled by hereditary strongmen. I recall those days of oil prosperity: weekends in Mexico City exploded into libertine festivals; the latest model cars, at that time especially the black Grand Marquis, sped down the downtown streets and parked in front of wild nightclubs. Bottles of champagne, cognac and whiskey were thrown out the windows of those cars at the barefoot, the voices within those autos alternating between drunken women and contented entitled men.

And from that moment on the country has been possessed by the plague of drug trafficking and the structures of power permeated by hot money, but nobody dares say so. At some tabloid daily where I worked when I first got to Mexico, the director would come to the office drunk at night and throw dollars in the air so the editors and employees would crawl on their hands and knees to scoop them up to the laughter of his immensely fat body guards with faces identical to those great Olmec heads. Colombian drug traffickers, no doubt accomplices of the local police, appeared floating rotting in the waters of the Tula River. At that time a person who was like some character out of a Valle Inclán novel, the famous Negro Durazo, named general by his childhood friend, the president, headed a pyramid that extorted millions of capital residents. On every street corner police brandishing machine guns fell upon passers-by, whom they kidnapped and only freed after the payment of cash ransoms that varied according to the case. No one was safe from the arbitrary acts, neither the rich nor the poor, neither professionals nor housewives. Tourists were extorted, women raped, total impunity reigned, just as in Alfred Jarry's work *Ubu Roi.* I was arrested, really kidnapped, one night and ended up in the famous holding cells of Tlaxcoaque, thrown amidst punks with shaved heads and beautiful transvestites who protected me while I slept on a concrete slab. The president was crying after nationalizing the banks and accused those who had sacked the nation, the same ones who over the previous few weeks had taken all their dollars out of the country. During those horrible days I carried the memory of Malcolm Lowry's *Under the Volcano* and D.H. Lawrence's *The Plumed Serpent,* the first a story about an arbitrary reign and a desolate corpse left with his pockets picked, and the other a drama of knife fights and murders.

I know that in a few days I'll return to Mexico City and see bankrupt small businessmen choked by high interest rates and long lines of happy credit card holders — the contemporary human I.D. card — ready to cover the interest of the money lenders or crying because their car or refrigerator has been repossessed. There will be explanations, suicides, sacrificial lambs and the masses will return to the calm of silence and slavery. The same silence from the Río Bravo to Patagonia, because this isn't only the situation in Mexico.

Sitting before the plaza, under the splendid sun and in the fresh breeze, the only real fortune we residents of this earth can count on, I find myself immersed again in the traditional ambience of Hispano-American literature, what we enthusiastically ate up during our adolescence in the Andean highlands. Juan Rulfo, Carlos Fuentes and Jorge Ibargüengoitia in the '60s showed us the reality of their country; one with a sad ancestral aesthetics, another with a lucid and exacerbated prose, the last with sarcasm, irony and humor. Just a few years ago, during the times of yuppie hysteria, it was said that Latin American literature was plagued by telluric themes like dictatorship, the *caudillo, Doña Barbara* and guerrillas which had gone out of fashion. In its place a few new authors tried to imitate the "impure" North American prose, dreaming they were already treading the paths of the First World. And now, barely a few years before the end of the millenium, less than two hundred years after Independence, here I am on the Guatemalan border in one more episode from the recurring literary material of the twentieth century's Big Daddies.

In 1981, on my first serious assignment as a correspondent, I was terrified when I went to the Chiapanecan city of Tapachula, dominated by the Lucas García brothers, before crossing into Guatemala. Thousands of Indians were massacred by the terrible *kaibiles* and members of the opposition were found quartered near the market places. It was dangerous for young people to wander about at night. That was the first time I visited Chiapas. Later I went to El Salvador where things were at a climax after the assassination of Archbishop Romero: at the luxurious Hotel Camino Real, on Boulevard of Heroes, they gave me a T-shirt that read, "Don't shoot. I'm a journalist." Jesuits priests at the Universidad Centroamericano, who were later assassinated, told me that if I wanted to truly see the horror I had to go to the Killing Fields near the volcanoes and I took a taxi there in the midday heat. Vultures devoured hundreds of rotting corpses. Photographers moved around the skeletons and skulls to get a better picture. Women, rebels, little children, old men were dumped there by the truckful, like in some Nazi death camp. I couldn't eat for three days. I suffered terrible paranoia. It was the most difficult and painful image of my life. Never had I seen so many bodies together, rotting upon the black volcanic lava as if there were nothing to it. At night all we could do was listen to rock music in the luxurious hotel bar while gringo journalists walked through the lobby with bottles of whiskey. Then I went to Honduras, Nicaragua, Costa Rica, Panama. Farcical elections, contras, revolutionary nuns, Protestant fanatics in the Tegucigalpa plaza, arrogant Sandinista *comandantes* and alluring *comandantas* in olive green uniforms like goddesses out of some adventure movie, a salsa dance attended by street corner thugs one unforgettable night in the Panama Canal Zone.

Revolutions come and go and nothing happens. Revolutionaries grow old and become rich and fat, with cynical cinematographic smiles and gold rings. The same story as always with the theme of death and messianic rhetoric. For every ex-guerilla gorged on champagne and salmon there are 30,000 dead innocents who gave their life for some foolish cause. Such classic themes are recurrent and will return to be treated by the children and grandchildren of Valle Inclán, Rivera y Gallegos, Asturias, García Márquez, Carpentier, Roa Bastos and Vargas Llosa. Bishops, *caudillos, caciques,* guerrillas, soldiers, Indians, speeches, politicians in neckties, Tuesday siestas, Big Mamas and Big Daddies, rebel generals, all in a colorful parade are as alive today as they were in the nineteenth century and they will survive no doubt with even greater intensity in the twenty-first. The masquerade of the First World is concentrated only in a few neighborhoods of potentates well guarded by security, while around them millions of citizens sit in agony before their televisions listening to news about the stock market and ads about the marvels of American Express. We live in the reign of pragmatism: the poor are not only stupid, they're wrong, their reasoning makes no sense. And any intellectual who tries to express a criticism of that world of numbers is qualified immediately by the intellectuals in power as a terrorist, nostalgic for Castro, anachronistic, a budding assassin.

The fall of the Berlin Wall made a few people lost in illusion believe that revolution had ended and affirmed for others the idea of the end of history and the triumph of market ideology. Like a signpost of so many things, this knowledge came to me at the southern tip of Manhattan, still full of dirty crazy homeless people living in the street, before the Republican mayor Rudy Giuliani arrived and converted the areas I used to frequent into pretty little streets for tourists. That icy November afternoon in 1989, we were devouring the early edition of *The New York Times* and the newspapers that came from Europe that dawn. Everything seemed normal for the people coming and going in Greenwich Village, on one side the habitués of Sweet Basil's and on the other side those of the Blue Note or the Village Gate, where Tania Maria had just finished her set. For any observer it was an extremely important day and the television images were revealing. In April of 1975 I had found myself talking about the fall of Saigon with a few friends in a restaurant by the Petit Palais in Paris. Now we were discussing such a change on Sixth Avenue. We were all excited about the news and devoured the analyses: we were watching the turning wheel of history, the grand theater of history.

Within a hundred years all these things we're so worried about will perhaps be just a few little chapters in some history book which much later in time will become nothing. But that's our nature: we have the right to get worked up in this short passage through the world which is life, just as we get worked up over love, desire, hate, vanity, ambition, bitterness, frustration, failure, sorrow. For thirty years the Berlin Wall seemed eternal, for seventy-two years the Soviet Union seemed invincible: now, as upon other tectonic plates of history, is the world truly living through another Renaissance or only more agony?

Tuesday, December 27

THE FIRST THING today is the arrival of Cardinal Adolfo Suárez and four bishops who will hold a conclave with the polemical "Bishop of the Devil." After meeting in the rectory, they all appear in the chapel of the Immaculate Conception where some twenty Tzotzil Indians in their typical garb wait, ready to play for them harp music accompanied by maracas and small drums. They have set out candles and offerings of fruit, sugar cane, oranges and incense that wafts a fragrant smoke between the conglomeration of the blessed. There is an obese bishop, coincidentally named Obeso, and other skinnier ones led by the trembling, timid Cardinal Suárez, who is surprised by the Indians when they bring him a maraca and invite him to dance and sing. The bishops came only to pronounce a few words to start the peace process and instead end up forced to dance to a sing-songy melody repeated over and over for more than half an hour.

The prelates are obviously fatigued and discomfited, jumping around and stirring the enthusiasm of the musicians and the photographers who have just heard about the surprising spectacle and like rats and cockroaches emerge from their dens of boredom and burst into the chapel to cover the scene and "make news." Suárez is sweating and his hands tremble. He's dressed in a gray secular suit and a little white priest's collar. The astute Bishop Ruiz takes advantage of the opportunity to speak to the Indians in their own language. He has spent days fasting, but looks stronger and more radiant than ever.

The Zapatistas salute the "government's decision" to accept the famous Comisión Nacional de Intermediación, with Bishop Ruiz presiding as mediator in the supposed dialogue. He plans to change his "prolonged fast" for a "liturgical" one while humanitarian caravans are enlisted to enter Zapatista territory with food supplies, and people flutter about at the seat of the "government in rebellion" installed in the local National Institute of Anthropology while military vehicles cross back and forth along the highways. There sits the governor in rebellion Amado Avendaño, the opposition candidate in the August '94 elections who was supported by the Zapatistas. He is a stout, swarthy man from the coast, a lawyer of lost causes, editor of the newspaper *El Tiempo,* an example of independent journalism far removed from government intrigue and corruption. A few Mexican dailies changed their point of view after the rebellion, but before this took place, Avendaño set an example with his precarious journal during the times these lands were forgotten and nobody heard their voice.

Now, near the market in the heights of the city, this "government" sends out dispatches and of course it's striking the ingenuity of a few partisans who have just discovered the exhilaration of confronting the powerful. One will never know if Avendaño won or lost the election, but what's for sure is that he's here representing a part of the conflict, the voice of the defeated. From his office emerge communiqués that almost nobody listens to, there gather those who wish to take provisions to the Zapatistas and from there leave the humanitarian caravans. When he decided to declare himself governor in rebellion, he said he was following in the steps of the nineteenth-century Mexican president Benito Juárez, who governed from a carriage on the move, who confronted the invader, who shot Maximiliano and is considered the father of the nation and a member of the Americas' Legion of Honor: the Indian from Oaxaca who achieved power and who, disgracefully, Benito Mussolini was named for.

Not far from here is the border with Oaxaca, another splendorous Mexican state. I first discovered it through the prose of the Oaxacan writer Vasconcelos and later I visited several of its villages. Its capital has a seductive colonial air with spectacular churches like San Felipe Neri, whose walls still carry the marks of old gun shots and the place where it's said Juárez was married, and Soledad and its strange colored stone on a little plaza where they hold the famous *Guelaguetza* dances. Not far from there is the house of Porfirio Díaz and on every corner you perceive another world yet to be devoured by modernity and its vain plastic utilitarianism. And dominating the entire valley are the ruins of Monte Albán, which I have visited so often, a few times drunk on good mezcal, a place where the afternoon clouds are within your reach.

Oaxaca is a country within the country and it's not strange that from its lands come such illustrious men as Díaz, Juárez, and the painter Tamayo. Vasconcelos guided me through the market, constructed at the end of the last century with the metallic Eiffel designs within which you witness an explosion of colors and smells, perceptions of a deep Latin America. I have walked down its streets, touched time there with my hands and witnessed the first visit ever of a Spanish monarch, King Juan Carlos I, to the indigenous lands of Mexico. He walked down those streets with his air of a popular king and big-nosed Bourbon face, swarmed by little kids, accompanied by his Greek wife Sophia. I was by him when he climbed Monte Albán, explored the miracle of the church of Santo Domingo with its golden altars, planted a tree next to an enormous millenary *tule,* danced the *Guelaguetza* and went to a village of weavers whose streets were covered by flowers. The governor, a man of indigenous origin named Heladio, waits for him at the town entrance. The king arrives and several short, plump Tehuana Indian women dressed in their colorful *hupiles* take him, decidedly, by each arm and walk to the central square. The governor is furious and orders them to let go of the monarch, who in turn takes hold of the women's arms and continues on, happy to be in their company. Five centuries after the discovery, the first king of Spain visits Oaxaca, a late date of the crown with these lands that still today fascinate us, part of this centuries-old mosaic that churns, fades away, returns, shines, turns dark. Further on I see some dance stages especially set up for the monarch and from one of them they throw big hard tortillas called *totopos* that fall near the retinue. People drink and eat; the Spanish functionaries look disconcerted, dressed in their impeccable suits, shirts and neckties. Suddenly the king, wearing a guayabera, takes a piece of tortilla and eats it to the crowd's laughter and then all the functionaries have to pick up off the ground a piece of tortilla and eat it while the king watches.

I walk through the streets of San Cristóbal beneath this splendid sun. For novelists and poets these are moments apt for letting the imagination run wild or releasing ideas from that strange machine, the brain. Writers are necessary, I think, which is why I disagree when it's said they proliferate on our continent or are an unstoppable pest. Those who indeed proliferate are politicians, academics, soldiers, priests, lawyers, journalists and the other species of diverse stripe that have in general caused all the great maladies of the Latin American continent. Their absurd rhetoric about radiant futures and limitless progress have brought all of us to the precipice: when I hear a politician still say we are colonies exploited by foreigners and must search for national liberation in order to find paradise, I tremble; there is nobody more evil, corrupt and cruel than our own rich; nobody more blind, soulless and stupid than our own yuppies. Money has always dominated the contemporary world, if we understand by that the last eight-thousand years. It's already a cliché the certainty that all our evils don't come from bad outside sources but from the very human nature of ambition and disloyalty. It's not true that when "we manage our own destinies" we will finally reach those dreams of stability and equality. It would be necessary to render account of all the evils we've committed ourselves and realize that foreign powers who have come here were almost always brought in by locals. Now our own neck-tied presidents are just little employees of that world-wide force of wealth.

There are very few of us writers in these lands because to maintain not only such an attitude about writing but also an ardent sensibility, you have to be heroic. Beginning in school the poet is always suspect; at home the news of this tendency is usually received like a death in the family, and later the young poet has to resist the temptations of power and money and the absurd idea of giving up this activity for just a little while to devote himself to a "real job" and save up to later return to writing. I have seen many people of my generation who didn't have the valor to go on and instead became lawyers, doctors, politicians, businessmen, cultural functionaries and so snuffed out their delirium.

Now, when I walk these streets beneath this sun out of some tropical novel, I remain even firmer today in the same disdain for politicians and professionals I felt in my adolescense. This continent survives in spite of them and if there is a brotherhood that can still provide force and vital sap it is artists in general and among them writers who create the imaginary, who mold it, speak it, throw it into the streets and minds where it palpitates, that brotherhood still concerned with rain, the color of flowers, the grace of hummingbirds, the sound of streams, the clear silhouette of a volcano, the aroma of vegetables: incredulous men and women who don't believe in the preachers of "democracy" or the merchants of revolution and on the contrary pray and search in sacred texts.

The poet and novelist would be the greatest accomplice of that population which out of the force of their simplicity is the wisest and truest, and for that same reason the least predatory. And in these crepuscular years of the century we are called to enjoy the creation of novels and poems which are not only nutrients of eccentricity in a utilitarian epoch, but proof of the transcendence, the certainty that there is great beauty in Baroque churches and sacred millenary words.

I love being lost: I saved myself from being a lawyer, a politician, a cultural bureaucrat and I continue in the happiness and sorrow of writing, with no possible return to the land of shopkeepers. I love writing for nothing and for no one, because it's reward enough just to do it. It seems terrible to me the life of those individuals who were once touched by the malady of literature and never decided to pursue it or gave up too quickly and now carry the burden of not having taken things to the limit. Besides a judicious hominoid, I am without doubt a writer and moreover a Latin American and I take pride in my literary ancestors like Rubén Darío, Julio Herrera y Reissig, Felisberto Hernández and Jorge Luis Borges, among so many others, those old forefathers who loved these lands and were generous to them and their people.

In my case the formation began in childhood, due to my father, who although didn't write any work himself was impassioned by language. Like so many Colombians of his epoch, formed in the decade of the '30s, his illusion was books. When he discerned that his twelve-year-old son was infected by literature, he helped him all he could from that point on. For that reason literature is sacred to me. The true writer tries to reveal himself and reveal other things, to illuminate and be illuminated, sure all the while that he belongs to an ancient brotherhood. At home I have many books from my father's library. With him I discussed the changes in fortune of their characters and their epoch and with him I shared the pleasure of poetry and its meaning. When he died he had two of my novels on his desk. I think he passed away with the surety that his son was a writer ready to take his vocation to the end, without any fissure of doubt.

A literary vocation cannot flower without a proper milieu and mine was the strange city of Manizales, dominated during the '50s and '60s by a Greco-Latin spirit and thus filled with anachronistic poets, nihilist rebels, and discomposed philosophers. My paternal grandparents were from Sonsón and my maternal grandparents from Santa Rosa de Osos, so I come from a typical family from the Antioquia region, linked to stories of the mountains, the *cordillera* mist, and now to the dislocations caused by drug trafficking and the mythical Pablo Escobar. The land of Tomás Carrasquilla and storytellers like Cosiaca and Montecristo is also key for the narratives and fables they told. I was lucky enough to have a dozen teen-age friends interested in the classics with whom I lived during those years in a world filled with idols like Cervantes, Wilde,

Whitman, Shakespeare, Dostoievsky, Rimbaud, Baudelaire and José Asunción Silva. Meeting in old drawing rooms down wood-floored corridors filled with flowers was a custom that nourished our youth and, no doubt, still persists in our beings because childhood is the true material of literature. In such an ambience is the gulf that nourishes writing.

As for travel, like all those in Manizales inflicted by literature, the dream was Paris and I had the fortune of destiny placing me there shortly after I turned twenty. In Paris I learned to know myself as a professional foreigner, to flee from nationalisms and the pettiness of literary parochialism, to respect people of every race and creed and always try to learn something from them. To live at such an age in that marvelous city charged with history was something brutal, stirring, key in my education. There I devoured fragments from one of the most fascinating bodies of world literature and for that reason I am an absolute literary Francophile: Rousseau, Abbé Prévost, Stendhal, Balzac, Flaubert, Proust, Céline, Apollinaire offer unforgettable experiences, especially when read in France.

Later I left for California and lived a transformative period in San Francisco and the Bay area, where I detoxified myself of Parisian life as a light-filled world opened for me: the Pacific Ocean, the Californian luminosity, book stores full of new unknown things, the ruins of the rock of Janis Joplin and Jimmy Hendrix in Berkeley and Haight Ashbury, contemporary North American literature, the gay apogee before AIDS, in the end another form of viewing literature and life through more pragmatic writers and innovative poets in an atmosphere that had nothing to do with Hispanic and Latin American rhetoric. I wrote a lot in a house on Virginia Street in North Berkeley, and searched for a literary path I would later exploit in Mexico.

A Latin American today must experience his language in the great cities of its various idioms and so I came to Mexico City as part of that adventure, that sentence of being a professional foreigner. It was very difficult, because one might think that in Mexico, where Spanish is spoken, the rules are the same as those in the West. Malcolm Lowry and D.H. Lawrence taught us that Mexico is also an exciting nightmare. But rather we should consider it a fascinating Oriental country, one that confronts us with the difficult challenge of living amidst veils and customs, specters of pre-Hispanic monsters and colonial phantoms in a tense relation with an indecent modernity. The enjoyable masks of lies and simulation refine one's literary weapons. Many writers of the world find themselves compelled there to write like mad: a veritable orgy only possible in a capital of the Spanish language like Mexico City, where our idiom is alive with its Babel-like pre-Hispanic and vice-regal mixtures, converted into a banquet of meanings for the maker of words. Conversations with Mexicans of my generation, the antique book sellers, the vibrant indigenous world, the food, the liquor, the cantinas, the solitude within the city, the pyramids have been key to my literary career.

Poetry is the truest and most flexible instrument for expressing the self through words. The most important aesthetic literary discoveries in the world, and in Latin America especially, have been accomplished by its poets. Throughout history poetry has been an act of complete rebellion, an act of alienation, a bet on failure and truth. Our epoch's cult of success and money can only be battled by poetry and I believe that the intense current aggression by images, news, advertising and the empty words of politicians is leading people back to poetry and nature. Journalism in its contemporary version, on the contrary, is an absolute catastrophe, a devouring leviathan of the instant operating through newspapers, radio and television that prevents us from being able to take repose and think, to ruminate about truth, about night and day. I don't believe in the need for news.

I have spent almost my entire adult life outside of my country. Still, I have always had a strong contact with Colombia through friends, the press, literature and trips back and I am convinced of an obvious Colombianicity whose most notorious characteristics are murder, the rumba, ambition and irreverence. The country I left in 1974 has changed quite a bit and no doubt there are many things of a sociological, ethnological and political order I don't understand for not living there. But I perceive that we Colombians have a right to end the disrespect for life and establish a country where our differences can be dissolved in a civilized manner and not by the methods imposed by the minorities of terror and the elite.

Regarding literature, we Latin Americans have to draw a map of our tradition, of course, but in this field we are part of a wider Hispano-American context and so must establish a dialogue with the other countries of the continent, as if we were all provinces of a splendid ambience: Castilian. That's why I love being a professional foreigner with multiple references. I would suffocate under a single nationalism, with its fixed local heroes and sacred nationalist history.

Wednesday, December 28

AN ENTHUSIASTIC group forms a line to receive their credentials as they prepare to travel with provisions to Guadalupe Tepeyac. Collaboration is required for that government to become legitimate and those in charge call each other *compañero* like during the distant '70s in Latin America. Here are a bunch of young women, some of them quite lovely and notable for their tall physique, whom I have seen lately walking around San Cristóbal in the sun. People you pass at the parish house, at City Hall, at the newspaper stand, in a bookstore, at a restaurant that you end up greeting without knowing their names, as if you all belonged to that "humanitarian brotherhood." They're carrying backpacks, they're wearing military boots, jeans, cotton shirts, they've got long hair, colorful woven bracelets, wide-brimmed hats. They run from place to place worried they'll lose their spot on one of the buses and get impatient, despite everybody knowing the departure will be delayed. Nothing to be done.

I take a taxi back to the plaza. In the cool air of the hotel restaurant, I watch the movement through a tinted window. I read the special edition of the magazine *Biblioteca* dedicated to, on the occasion of his centenary, the Frenchman Ramón Fernández, father of the writer Dominique

Fernández, whom I once met at his country's embassy in Mexico City during a cocktail party attended by local writers. Ramón was the son of a Mexican diplomat and a French woman who grew up in France without links to Mexico, a country he was ashamed of as an adult. The elder Fernández became an important essayist and critic with the first generation of the *Nouvelle Revue Française,* a writer whose work is almost completely unknown in Spanish. According to the magazine, among his books figure *Messages, Vie de Molière* and the novels *Le pari* and *Les violents,* as well as *L'homme, est-il humain?* He was a friend of Proust, Gide, and Drieu la Rochelle and lived out the conflicts of his generation between the temptations of communism and fascism, finally adhering to the latter and becoming a collaborator in occupied Paris. He died in 1944, before the liberation, sparing himself from the judgment and contempt flung at other collaborators such as Louis Ferdinand Céline and Drieu la Rochelle, who committed suicide before being brought to justice.

This strange character was now receiving a tribute from a country he had always rejected, it seems, from the influence of his French grandmother, who was quite unhappy that her grandson had roots in that strange country on the other side of the ocean. In a moving and lucid special text in *Biblioteca,* his son Dominique says this rejection "has to be considered less an intellectual decision than an intimate conflict of a psychological nature," and recalls that his grandmother "never spoke of either her Mexican husband nor her stays in Mexico," because after the death of her husband she had "a deep, ferocious fight" with his family and from then on held "an implacable disapproval" of them. On the cover of the magazine is a picture of the man and inside photos where he is seen with the undoubtable features of an *amateur sudaméricain.*

A strange destiny for this man of Mexican origin, afflicted by hard alcoholic episodes, who collaborated with the Nazis and was seduced by the Hitlerian madness like many others, among them innumerable Latin Americans. Sitting here in this restaurant, it seems curious that chance makes me take pleasure in the prose of this character whose inner tension must have been terrible: to have savage, aboriginal blood for which, no doubt, the Nazis would have condemned him to the gas chamber, and to be more of a papist than the Pope in his right-wing nationalism when finally as an adult he had to change his indisputable Mexican nationality and became a French citizen. I read his text "Poetics of the Novel," in which he expresses some original ideas about the genre, among them that the novel is a kind of "integral calculus of concrete knowledge" or "the dramatic analysis of living man."

Biblioteca is one of Mexico's best literary magazines and here I am enjoying it in San Cristóbal de las Casas, where you find just about everything. Dominique Fernández recounts how as he got older he finally broke that thread his family had led him by, distancing himself from them even more after a chance encounter some twenty-five years ago with a wicked Mexican relative who looked him up in Paris that he didn't like for his bourgeois pretensions. And in truth I understand him, because there is nothing worse than a Latin American with airs of being rich and aristocratic. These people with a complete lack of sensitivity and no sense of the ridiculous: they treat waiters and "servants" badly with their boundless *arrivisme*, they look at dark-skinned people with disdain although they're dark-skinned themselves, believing they're blue-bloods although they've been mix-blooded for light years. This descendent of Fernández had to contend with being such a specimen and remained traumatized for it. At that cocktail party where I met and spoke briefly with him he seemed rather shy, but the atmosphere was pleasant, thanks to the ambassador at the time, Alain Rouquié, an intellectual with experience in Latin America who didn't host those tedious drawn-out receptions full of stupid government officials. His timidity expresses that rather strange relation between Europe and Latin America. At least in regard to literature and thought, the Latin America intellectual class is completely European. They all grow up sucking at the teat of the antique and modern classics of various nationalities. Many Latin American intellectuals speak French, German, Portuguese, Italian or English and in some cases are as well or better versed than the natives in their respective literary histories

Ramón Fernández, a pro-Nazi collaborator, is a strange case, because at his time there were great Hispanicists in France, among them the genial Valéry Larbaud, as well as Don Alfonso Reyes, who spoke about his ancestors that lately I have seen walking around in the San Cristóbal sun. There are no worse enemies of Latin America than those who deny it due to their own personal issues. During my years in Paris and the United States I was amused to see Latin Americans who wouldn't associate with others, as if out of pride. The poor man rendered homage by *Biblioteca* really looks Latin American, but I suppose he couldn't stand being a dark-skinned native from a land of Indians. The mother contributed to deepening the trauma and not even the Mexican homage can make up for it. Only his son, still lost in this world on the other side of the sea, tries to return and establish contact with his origins and for that reason, among others, he baptizes his son Ramón, so the name will not be lost.

Through the window I see go by the woman doctor with the contorted face. She has a special grace and is surrounded by admiring cameramen, who along with the photographers enjoy a lot of success around here. At this point reporters, including war correspondents, have already been displaced by photographers and cameramen, who with just a few images or a sole photo can say everything that occurs anywhere. With time they will remain, no doubt, the only survivors of the profession of journalism and this seems just to me. Written journalism in general should disappear because it is monstrous bastard genre of language. Outside of poetry words are useless. The young doctor is right to pass pompously before the cameramen and photographers, the athletic emotional vanguard of today's journalism.

The image is transparent in order to communicate. I remember the night CNN transmitted live to the world the attack on the Palace of Congress by order of Boris Yeltsin, czar of the end of the century, no doubt soon to be forgotten by history for not having during some big drunk launched an atomic bomb at Paris or New York or created a genocidal system to eliminate millions of rebel nationalists. That night I couldn't sleep, stuck to my television, and I spent the next day waiting for the attack, eventually produced before the cameras with explosive emotion. I also recall the first view of the Persian Gulf War, broadcast as well by that network in living color, lights from the missiles flashing in the air during that Baghdad night. These images have become a new form of aesthetic pleasure for millions and millions of television viewers throughout the world, more concrete than poetry, more profound than painting.

The precursor image to all this was the arrival of man to the moon on July 20, 1969, which I watched with my family on an archaic television inside a fine wooden console, beside an old patio filled with primroses and azaleas in a house on 19th Street in Manizales. News agencies will disappear, newspapers are becoming more and more anachronistic: for the elect population of the monstrous and inevitable elitist world of *Blade Runner* will be the information superhighway, where beside your morning coffee will be invoked a daily journal from any place in the world, instantaneously, on the all-powerful, omniscient, omnipotent, omnivorous computer screen. What's happening is neither bad nor good, it is. Nothing is forever. The cameramen, the Indians, the Bishop, the astronaut Neil Armstrong, the anonymous soldiers, the tourist, Subcomandante Marcos, none of us live forever.

But let's return to the theme of rebellion, suddenly prompted by Señor Fernández and the magazine *Biblioteca*. Every generation confronts the dichotomy between resignation and rebellion and there will always be those who fight for the first and others who fight for the right to oppose the establishment and its laws. In the first camp will be those who stoically opt for patience and still others will try to impose waiting as the weak's only option in face of the powerful, with whom they are complicit: the weak in rebellion must be punished, annihilated, for their acts result in chaos and depart from the "right" that legitimizes the impunity of the wealthy. In the second camp will be those who rebel from some avid messianic impulse for power and glory and whose megalomaniac path will take them to the farthest extremes. The hero becomes the infallible one who condemns to the firing squad or gallows those who oppose his designs: "everything within the revolution, nothing outside of it," "fatherland or death," "we'll sooner drown ourselves in the sea than hand over our infallible ideology, my ideology, my obsession," says the tropical tyrant, in this case Fidel Castro, who has already become an old patriarch that prefers the island drown than be governed by someone besides himself.

The rebellion we are witnessing in these millenary lands of Chiapas doesn't seek, paradoxically, power and in that sense it is something new: they have taken up arms in order to put an end to their compatriots' cowardly and complicit resignation in face of the ruling party's tyrannical officials and their imposition of neoliberalism, whose obstinacy is comparable to the tyranny of Castro and other totalitarians of the recent past: "free enterprise or death," "we'll sooner drown ourselves than renounce our path of progress toward the First World," they say, no longer dressed like soldiers but stock brokers. For them the Indians are wrong because they don't want to eat McDonald's hamburgers, they're mistaken because they don't use shampoo and don't want Campbell soup, they're stubborn because the women wear traditional dress instead of what's in fashion and still braid their hair instead of getting it done at a salon. To turn your back on progress is to be wrong.

During the desolation of the past decade I thought, like many other children of the post-'68 generation with its marginal rebellions, that the desire for liberty and justice had been lost forever and that neoliberalism and the extreme Protestant, Puritan, Calvinist idea of success and usefulness had finally triumphed atop the ruins of the Berlin Wall and totalitarianism. As for us, the defeated Romantic post-hippies, we had been expulsed from that paradise of impresarios and zombies out of George Orwell's novel *1984* or Fritz Lang's film *Metropolis.* Outside of the stock exchange reality doesn't exist for them, it's all just a mistaken world of myth and magic realism. Such a frightening ideology triumphed over the world with Reagan and the English "iron lady" Margaret Thatcher and their worldwide technocracies, converted into the new crusaders of the Holy Grail. In our countries all the little presidents of venture capital, executives who had never read a book in their lives nor looked beyond their noses of cheap little political hacks, absorbed the doctrine and began parroting it. And as in their own time the Nazis had a court of intellectuals and writers, many writers of the continent fell into the trap and became more Catholic than the Pope: according to them, prisoners of an inexplicable and hypnotic historical amnesia, the idea of revolution had finally ended, the pariahs had to give up, all rebellion was the incarnation of evil, to talk of the poor was to be totalitarian, a Stalinist, dogmatic, a terrorist.

Now in this great country of Mexico in ancient colonial lands near El Salvador — until recently victims of their own holocaust, which fortunately ended with the Cold War — and Guatemala, where the disgusting white aristocracy still aspires to exterminating the Indians, they are quite late in taking a position about a problem we other Latin American countries have already lived through: on one side are the perfumed intellectuals who request the tacit elimination of the insolent Indians manipulated by white ideologues, those Indians who slap them in the face with a lost guerrilla struggle, Indians who shame North Americanized Mexico and, on the other hand, those intellectuals who defend the weak and who were immediately demonized, as during the years of McCarthyism in the United States in the 1950s, by the chiefs of infallible neoliberalism and free commerce, the only panaceas they say are left to the region at the turn of this new millenium.

It's astonishing how history repeats itself: David against Goliath, Christ against the Pharisees, the crucified and the powerful, wise men and prophets who unblushingly defend the homicidal and corrupt tyranny with obvious muteness and so receive their stipends. The surging myth of Marcos and the Zapatista rebels was unexpected and its effects on the mass media weren't planned for because conditions seemed the same as in the past. For the hero to emerge there has to be an unmovable, infallible, stubborn and obtuse force, the masses and intellectual class resigned to cowardice and defeat, in a certain form corrupted, and no longer able to dream or question; on the margins an unexpected enlightened one decides to do what his contemporaries are incapable of: give up his life for a cause.

Those are the elements that an unexpecting country and world, avid for a hero, were waiting for, as occurred with Christ in his time and since then has continued with so many others and will continue century after century until this planet comes to an end. You have to be a little naïve to believe that rebellion is anachronistic: it transcends time and is part of human nature. It will exist as long as man does. Rebellion exists now and always will, despite the songs and festivals in honor of its imminent end. Jesus, Bolívar, Joan of Arc, Che Guevara, Nelson Mandela, and on the other side the mythic Caligula, Herodes, Reagan, Hitler, Pol Pot, who will also continue to exist because they are necessary characters in this human history of the good and the bad on Planet Earth. Every generation comes to understand this after suffering through rebellion and resignation, cults of power and cults of weakness. Every generation is condemned to discover its own tepidness.

Thursday, December 29

TODAY WAS another day of poems. Poetry isn't a profession, a duty, an obligation. The poem emerges when it's least expected from some inner need, like a drop of water springing from a rock, erupting from distant magmas and passing through the filter of such varied mineral veins. The poem is a pure, or impure, drop of water on a cavern wall that finally falls, provoking multiple sounds in the humid expanse. It's useless to search for the words, which come when least expected; the poem knocks at the door, it comes with its own rhythm, grace, disgrace, or lack of grace. There lies its phantom upon the notebook, the loose leaf of paper, the napkin in a restaurant, there in the face of an unknown woman, a church, the rain. Despite all the horrible things I've said over the last few days about our continent — points moreover nobody would dare deny because they are irrefutable in their ignominy — I'm happy to take up poetry, one of the few windows left open to us, a presence which enlightens every corner of the Americas.

Poetry flourished in pre-Hispanic times. Coming on horseback from Tepoztlán to Amatlán de Quetzalcóatl earlier today, we passed by an immense door in a wall where, according to indigenous legend, lies the entrance to a secret world that opens every half-century. A few Mexicans used to bring their children to show them an enormous stone door drawn upon one of the mountains of the legendary Tepozteco, just fifty kilometers from infernal Mexico City, and they never doubted the certainty of the legend. Here nobody doubts the pre-Hispanic poetry and special editions by experts are published with texts saved from the slaughter of the Spanish conquest. The Mayan *Chilam Bilam* and *Popol Vuh,* the verses of Nezahualcóyotl, the copal of religious rites, the frescos, codices, pyramids, causeways, ruins, are words of stone and mud that still survive among this nation's inhabitants. In the colonial world the tradition continued, incarnated by Sor Juana Inés de la Cruz, who one imagines there in her cloister full of stars and planets.

Today poetry is one of this country's liveliest activities. As has occurred with the Chileans, Peruvians and Nicaraguans, Mexicans cultivate poetry and have forged a solid tradition that reaches its highest expression in the works of some of Los Contemporáneos from the first half of the twentieth century and in Octavio Paz, with his celebrated *Piedra de Sol, Ladera este, Blanco,* the poem "Nocturne of San Ildefonso" and those recent texts in "Árbol adentro," which many young people know by heart. The new poets – artists like Díaz Mirón, Tablada, González Martínez, Ramón López Velarde, Xavier Villaurrutia — not only exercise their passion but are translators of work from other languages, attempting to establish connections with other worlds as Paz did with the Orient.

There are of course great essays and prose, a great example the texture of José Vasconcelos' *Memoirs,* beginning with the splendid "Ulises criollo." But poetry is the sap of this country. I understand the indifference of many Mexican poet friends of mine to the political vicissitudes of their country: they are connected instead to the voice of springs and deserts, cacti and ardent rocks, parched walls painted blue and ochre resting in the dust, temples and colonial palaces. Their time, even now, is another time: the door of Amatlán de Quetzalcóatl still hasn't opened and when it does it will inaugurate another circular cycle. The Spaniard María Zambrano cites Nietzsche in the last volume of *The Agony of Europe:* "Everything deep needs a mask," and it is certain that the Mexican profundity needs masks and veils. Only poetic language, poetic speech, poetic knowledge can approach mystery and through those words one wanders between mirrors and is reflected among them in the labyrinth. Mexico is less Western than other countries of the Americas, fortunately. What it is living through now is the tension between the unexpected highway toward a forced Westernization that adopts some as its heirs and the voice of deep Mexico, with its masks.

I walk near the Cathedral and come across someone I've known for a long time. He works with the PRD, the center-left opposition party, and as with so many others, this is his first time here since the rebellion. He's a bit out of sorts, acting like someone who has just arrived. He buys boots. He'd like to play at adventure, but he doesn't know there is no adventure here. It's a war of "grand tourism" without bullets, a war of words, voices, masks, almost more profound than the typical war with thousands and thousands of dead bodies buried in mass graves.

But a stranger surprise is the encounter with the man I'll call the poet. He's someone I've seen many places since first arriving to Mexico, a figure in accord with the masks and mysteries. He reminds me of that character played by Linda Hunter in the movie "The Year of Living Dangerously." I hadn't seen him for awhile and it turns out he's from here. He takes me around to various churches, and at San Francisco I admire the impressive pulpit. We end up at the Casa de Cultura Jaime Sabines, named after a local poet linked to the ruling party whose poetry has achieved great popular success in Mexico: love poetry, confessional poetry, something primal with no relation to the abstract currents that extend from Sor Juana, pass through Díaz Mirón and Los Contemporáneos and end with Paz. I can't forget seeing Sabines one dawn in the Chamber of Deputies, in 1988, during the legitimization of Carlos Salinas de Gortari, a president who probably didn't win the election but was imposed by the system. It was sad to see the poet looking old and infirm, forced to rise at dawn and raise his hand among a flock of voters from the ruling party: the most anti-poetic thing possible one could imagine. But that's Latin America — when he's not wicked, the poet thrives and bows to the academics and officials. Sabines rose with difficulty from his seat, lifted his hand holding a little flag and voted in favor of what to all appearances was usurpation.

Now this beautiful cultural facility carries his name and I'm brought here by a poor, skinny, marginalized fifty-year-old eternally adolescent poet. He recites for me one of his poems. After decades of exile in the capital he has returned to his mother's side, with whom he lives in one of those houses with terra cotta tile roofs off which the rain flows. I am fascinated by damned young poets, by the poor poets who never could understand the laws of life and end up like the Verlaine of photos, with a face swollen by alcohol and a gaze made coarse from suffering, connected to the voice, that voice of what I was thinking about earlier. After these past few days, as I have tried to avoid journalists, it's a miracle to come across a fucking poet. I toast him with a shot of vermouth and later we walk through the streets of his childhood, the places where this poet carried his satchel with notebooks and pencils and watched late afternoon fall and played the trumpet and cried in desolation or laughed happily in the mists of forty years ago. We go into a typical local cantina called La Oaxaqueña, discussing the divine and the human. Now and then I have to go out and make a call on my cell phone or retrieve messages about what's going on, while inside the poet savors a delicious tequila.

A few hours later we stroll down the street a few blocks, a bit drunk. Some guy is walking along, holding the hand of a precious eight-year-old child, a blond boy with the air of an apparition whom the man got custody of after his divorce, according to what he tells us right after we greet him. The man is no doubt an indurate alcoholic, another damn artist in exile, and he offers me a necklace of polished obsidian flakes the boy wears around his neck. I buy it from him. The child looks at me; he is an angel from a post card who won't last here on earth more than a few hours or a few years. The sign is already there. I believe in amulets, encounters, in the voice, the door not yet open. The damn poet has time to give a piece of advice to the damn painter: "It's for your son — stop drinking."

We walk a block farther and at a beautiful hundred-year-old house the poet knocks on the portal. "This house belonged to my father," he exclaims and we enter a colonial atmosphere that reminds me of the *bahareque* mansions in my country, with their corridors and solitudes. A big playful whelp barks at the guy, grabs his silk scarf and runs off while the servants laugh. He doesn't pay any attention. In the back, sitting on a rickety chair, stirs a smiling old man almost a hundred years old, holding a Bible in his hands. He is happy to see the poet and hands him the book so he'll recite the Sermon on the Mount. The old man has a long white beard, an "authentic *coleto,*" as he is immediately qualified, his eyes covered with cataracts and possessing a happiness that transcends time, a strange puerile happiness that comes from beyond his death. The poet spits a bit while he reads and the old man in turn dribbles a little, enraptured by the pleasure of hearing the word of God in the voice of the bard, the son of his dead friend. Only a poet could bring me here to this damp old patio to stand before an old man from another century, who at one moment, while they prepare us a delicious cup of coffee, has time to bring us a newspaper with a speech of Subcomandante Marcos. I feel a certain anxiety. Time has stopped in the patio. Time from the past century. We urbane people get desperate in such peace; we like to be far from the truth, engaged in useless activity. We don't like to hear time checked or see death hiding in the shadows.

This night, after filing a few stories from the house we work out of on the outskirts of San Cristóbal, I return to the Casa de Cultura Jaime Sabines, where one of the many books about Chiapas is being presented, this time a collection of sociological and anthropological essays about the insurrection, rebellion, guerrillas, whatever they want to call it. A Frenchman with a long white beard wearing a poncho who has lived here for decades, André Aubry, is there. The academics read and discuss their papers and at the end the damn poet creates a scandal by denouncing the sociologists for supposedly mismanaging funds and other secret intrigues. Finally everything calms down.

We end up going to Santo Domingo, where a Mexican rock musician named Guillermo Briseño is giving a concert at a cultural fair organized by people from San Cristóbal. Local life goes on and they award prizes to young artists from the region, writers, poets, photographers, graphic artists. Some of the prize winners are young people who used to live in Mexico City or abroad but return here to spend time in the houses of their family, perhaps trying to recover their childhood. It's a simple affair, nothing official, at the little theatre in this former convent and I attend because I am one of them. Here, as in Valparaíso, Maracaibo, San Juan, Guayaquil, Manaos and the most diverse places on the continent is the living flame of art. The director of this cultural week, with exhibits of amber, photography, and paintings, says in the closing address they have lost money, but who cares, and they're all enthusiastic about the conferences, concerts and exhibits they've organized. It's bracingly cold and the air that reddens the cheeks of the young prize winners and the people of San Cristóbal reminds me of the same air in Colombia's cold lands. There as well, far from the folly of our politicians and petty despots, young people of every time and place hold parties like this and in such warmth Hispanic-American culture and art continues to grow: politicians and rulers pass away and art continues living. The artists who almost five-hundred years ago constructed the convent and church are here with us tonight. Of course this local event isn't news for anybody, not even the Mexican journalists, but here I feel connected with the authentic life of this place, shivering with cold in the old corridors of the marvelous former convent of Santo Domingo, built under the direction of Dominican monks in 1544.

The church is precious. Its exterior has the rustic features of the first churches on this side of the ocean. How many Indians worked during that distant sixteenth century, and how many died, for the reddish jewel to emerge that each afternoon is illuminated by twilight? It has as well strange balconies covered with terra cotta tiles and the former convent leads us back through the centuries. I have the custom of visiting these churches in each town I come to: before them I imagine their builders in a world that had just barely begun to form; I try to capture the adventurers and abbés from the other side of the sea in these half-wild depths of the New World, almost certain they would never return to their own lands. I hear the peal of the bells, the smoking, crackling wood fires, the canticles, the Sunday market. The ant hill of hundreds of artisans installed in the atrium on festival days, just like now. The Indians of different ethnic groups I see today with their goods are the same as five-hundred years ago: they wear the same clothes, they have identical faces and the same indifference to the modernity others try to force upon them, their children play and speak in millenary languages, unconcerned about the world of progress and consumerism.

When all at once you feel seized by time and land, you clearly understand the truth of the miracle of this passage on earth, the reward of seeing this sunset over the rustic church walls. Young tourists, indigenous mothers carrying children on their backs, silent old men. There's something in the light you can almost feel pulse. And then comes that unique instant of the writing of the poem. The poem as something organic, necessary, a vessel communicating between the unique being and the world in which he fades away.

Friday, December 30

IN THE MORNING I go to the church Our Lady of Carmen and there, next to a vast mansion in the typical Spanish style with wide corridors, at one time a convent or rectory, gather knaves disguised in good official style to inaugurate the Indigenous Pact, which bestows scholarships on sixteen people to study law. The journalists wait for the governor, but the first to arrive is the local writer Eraclio Zepeda, who seems a bit uncomfortable and nervous. He is considered by many, especially the Zapatistas and leftists, a horrible traitor who supports the illegitimate de facto imposed government.

Zepeda is a poet, a short story writer, a man with a great talent for words, whose oral stories are enjoyed in many parts. He's fat with a Mexican moustache and once acted as Pancho Villa in a film by the Russian director Bordanchuk. Zepeda is one of those legendary men of the left, travelers during the Cold War through the countries of Eastern Europe, lovers of Cuba, promoters of the Socialist cause, whom the radicals in Colombians call *mamertos,* ass-kissers, for they always get along well with governors and rulers. Great revolutionaries of language like Neruda, but *bon vivants* who wouldn't risk their lives for the cause they defend, much less live in the penury of a socialist country. Now he has accepted being named prime minister of the state of Chiapas, and over the last few days he has had to defend the advances of the army into rebel territory.

Journalists press around with useless agitation to listen to the words of governor Eduardo Robledo, as Zepeda listens at his side. The supposed Indians, who speak perfect Spanish and wear strange hats, seem as if they were bought off a long time ago and I suppose they're taken from one city to another to show the press there are Indians who favor the ruling party's administration. They have corrupted, cynical faces, but are dressed up there in front of Robledo and Zepeda to dramatize a caricature of the Indigenous Pact, signed behind closed doors but of course before all the cameras and microphones. The church has just been renovated and smells of freshly polished wood. The Baroque golden altars fade into the pale white walls.

I return this night to the Casa de Cultura Jaime Sabines. I've already had it with filing stories about a calm situation, a serious one, of course, but not meriting such a spread of information. I come here to be far from the intense clamor of everyone staying at the Hotel Casa Vieja. I agree with the Chilean painter Roberto Matta, who not long ago said that besides priests, the military and politicians, journalism is the plague of the twentieth century. I take refuge in the hall of poets and repose with a hot coffee and *rompope*.

This brief "cure" or "cleansing" in San Cristóbal has brought to mind certain things as I find myself again in a healthy solitude and delicious brisk weather, that solitude which is nice to prolong in order to find again those inner voices. Mexico City is so agitated and hostile with its daily hassles and street noise that there is no time to look at oneself from a distance, in order to know oneself. It is a horrendous city produced by the terrible Calvinist mistake of this century: the chimera of progress and development. You don't see the stars there, you don't know the late afternoon. Here certain twilights revindicate the use of that devalued word – they are true crepuscules; even more: splendorous, millenary crepuscules, and one feels the Church of Santo Domingo impregnated by them, bathed by a thousand twilights; those stones know it, covered by a vintage patina of setting suns. In this microcosm everything is clearer. A memory surges forth now: the cinematic desolation of San Andrés Larráinzar with those Indian women holding their bundled children, attentive to the discourse of a maskless Zapatista, and in the background other silent people waiting for the darkness, the clouds, the cold to arrive. The perfect atmosphere for a strange film whose theme would be precariousness, the total austerity of poverty. Concentrated as I am on this text, an intellectual-looking young woman watches me from another table. That clear gaze, looking strangely at the stranger, the outlander, a perfect beginning for a story. The stranger, the unknown, the traveler, the fellow man, the only lovable truth. Love always surges between unknown people.

Literature — so what? I've always thought in my case it is a personal impulse stemming from childhood, a pleasure, a complete necessity. The cults around certain authors, the naïveté of an idolatrous public, the blind ambition of certain writers to become famous or make money, seem pathetic to me. Gaping ambition, voracity, pettiness are proof they aren't writers; they are literati, as Juan Ramón Jiménez said at a conference in Miami at the end of the '30s. There are writers that write because they need to, others because it is their work, their profession. They could have been something else — lawyers, shopkeepers, botanists, hit men — but for some strange reason they fell into literature which tires them out with its desperation and lack of perspective. They don't know they will die and rot in their grave and that nothing nor nobody is saved from being forgotten, from becoming cosmic dust. Some day not a sole particle of this earth will be left and nobody will recall Greek vases, the blind Homer, Prospero, Virgil, Garcilaso de la Vega or Cervantes.

Years ago in San Francisco, perhaps May or June of 1980, I sat down to write in the pages of a diary in a café on Columbus Street near Ferlinghetti's bookstore City Lights. After Paris and Los Angeles I went to live in that marvelous city which surpasses any image one can imagine. First I lived at the Hotel Western, run by a Greek guy with the mentality of a kid, a man born in Alexandria, Egypt, and raised in an orphanage. At his hotel he only welcomed young adventurers of the world, no older than twenty-five or twenty-six, that he rented economical rooms, along with a breakfast pastry, in a kind of living arrangement that reproduced his years of childhood hospitality. When I ran out of money he told me it was no problem, I could stay there until I got another job, something I quickly managed to do at a U.S. Census office. My job was to telephone city residents and fill out questionnaires about them, by which I was able to practice my English and hear the fascinating stories of crazy people, desperate blacks, women who recalled their wartime lovers, proud homosexual couples, talkative Latinos, pastors of strange religions. The office consisted of some forty colleagues of every nationality, poor whites, Hindus, Koreans, Vietnamese, Salvadorans, Peruvians, Russians, Poles, and we hung out a lot together.

I used to love just walking all over San Francisco and enter any bookstore I came across, as has been my custom my whole life. The first books I read with fluency in English were the novels of Jerzy Kosinski, the prolific emigrant novelist who relates the horrors of the Holocaust, his experiences as a Jewish child of the Exodus, love stories on the straight highways of the southern United States, a man whose end it seems was suicide, accused of plagiarism by his enemies. I also went to bars and listened to *charanga, salsa* and rock and talked with all my friends. Mission Street was the Hispanic Tower of Babel in San Francisco, another sector of this American continent.

Around September of that year, after quite a few shots of tequila, I heard coming out of some place Mexican *ranchera* music sung by the voice of a tall, hefty woman wearing a colorful poncho, which made me ask myself: What am I doing in this country, rotting away where the only sign of life is the idea of making a buck? I took my money out of California Savings and a little bit more I had at the Bank of America and came to Mexico, where paradoxically I had more difficulties than ever when I first got here. Mexico was more mysterious to me than France or the United States; the first few months here almost drove me crazy, I didn't understand the enmeshed codes and strange veils everyone always wears, the difficulty of getting to the bottom of things. To live in Mexico one must become a monolith capable of having a subtle heart. Mexico was like trying to kick a stinging bee and it took me a long time to understand its tunnels and labyrinths, the secret dialogues that seem not to be so, the conversation of silence, the meanings of glances and smiles, the value of yes and no, the Churrigueresque nature of relations.

Only now is Mexico a world for me just a little less impenetrable, flowing over a screen filled with sphinxes, pyramids, oracles, voiceless voices, insoluble puzzles. A three-dimensional video. Virtual reality? Perhaps I know so many things about it that I've become impenetrable to myself, like those gazes that say nothing and say everything, like those police and bureaucrats in search of a bribe that ensnare the innocent in sinister exitless nightmares. I have lived that nightmare of the Mexicans, because the cruelty of the "system" doesn't only punish the foreigner, it does as well the native. The native has to learn to pass through these desolate labyrinths that offer neither shelter nor protection, sure of never finding the way out, threatened by the minotaur until he realizes his destiny is to be lost in those meaningless meanings, in those stoneless pyramids: the Mexican has had to learn the spiritual mumbo-jumbo in order to survive, walking over abysmal borders, at times seized by some unnamed strong-armed politician, other times alone in the exile of dismissiveness, other times in a desolate solitude, inert, dead to life. Everything can seem normal to the uninitiated: the streets full of people, the packed buses, the metro, the movies, the markets, the highways, the bustling city, the faces, but in the end it's all fiction, a big lie based on cruel certainties like the flag, pre-Hispanic myths, Baroque churches, democracy, justice, equality, an effective right to vote, national brotherhood, when it's all just words. Symbols? Meanings?

What a strange world this is I've fallen into, like so many other foreigners and so many other Mexicans. I've always affirmed my foreignness, because I haven't been able to keep quiet in face of such lies, fake colors, meaningless words, forced to kneel before the little despots, big paper tigers who shine atop slippery pyramids covered by moss and lichens. I don't know who is more lost, the trapped foreigner who ends up becoming a sphinx, a stone idol, a hardened spectator or the Mexican foreigner drowning in his mire, smashed by the stone of his fate, lashed drunk to a cantina table, impotent in face of secret power, while the music of old idols plays in the background.

What is a hero? Someone who undertakes the impossible and who to achieve his dream risks his life, and those of other people. At times he risks his life for pleasure and in that sense there is no sacrifice. The hero encounters forces that surpass his own, and so repeats the myth of David and Goliath. His surprising daring incites admiration and love, hate and jeering. Jesus spoke out strongly against the power of his time. The exceptional Joan of Arc dared the impossible being a woman, young and virgin, according to legend. Napoleon came from obscure origins and achieved glory at an early age. Bolívar still fascinates Latin Americans. Che Guevara is a kind of contemporary saint and the photo in which he appears dead glassy-eyed upon a table in Bolivia is a very localized Latin American version of Christ.

For this reason Subcomandante Marcos has become a hero who stirs emotions: he is young, genteel, the mask increasing his mystery; he is eloquent and witty, his impeccable voice even more impressive over the loudspeakers of his realm; he's an excellent writer when he tries, with a liberated prose exceptional among the writers of his generation and he knows very well the significance of his movement in relation to past actions. At times he's also corny and confusing, but at other times he is certain in his journalistic strategy. Since the first day of January of 1994 he has humiliated the ruling party, he has dragged into the mud the omnipotent presidential powers, he has shamed those Mexicans who have always submitted to power. Women see him as the most desirable man this country has had in many decades.

Marcos legitimizes his daring by recalling the memory of other heroes: on one hand Benito Juárez in the nineteenth century, the diminutive Indian who raised the flag of dignity and sent the invader Maximiliano to the firing squad, and on the other hand Emiliano Zapata, that other native son who rose up in Morelos during the period of the Porfirio Díaz regime against the power of the capital's scientific dandies. Women go crazy over Marcos, intellectuals hate and envy him but respect his seductive prose, impeccable when he wants it to be — witty, irreverent, even funny and self-mocking. He says to the four winds what every honorable Mexican should have wanted to one day say, but never dared out of fear of losing their job or ruining their political or diplomatic career. Marcos is a lucid megalomaniac who wins with his obvious failure. What true writer isn't a megalomaniac? Marcos says what he thinks, Octavio Paz says what he thinks, neither would say something ordered to them by someone else. Both are called to be followed, not to follow. To be loved or hated.

In the highlands of the Chiapas mountains, a Mexican hero has been born and only a year into his struggle, whether dead or alive, whether he disappears or sells out, whether or not he turns into some bureaucrat in a suit and tie, he will pass into history as an exceptional Mexican, uniquely capable of heading a valiant movement that humbly dared confront the all-powerful and infallible official party and its army. When he and the Zapatistas appeared to be surrounded, he developed a skillful strategy for returning to the front page of the newspaper. The great media outlets, which like consecrated priests today legitimize what occurs in the world, will be there waiting New Year's Eve and the first anniversary of the unthinkable, unheard of rebellion.

At this late date I look at everything like a spectator: I don't trust heroes. But the force of this movement resides in the fact it is formed of pure Indians, the authentic original inhabitants of these lands, the fathers of a nation that so often refers to its symbolic system in order to legitimize the power of the *Criollos*. The impotence of the government of young white technocrats is that it can't shoot those Indians playing war, aided by their indigenous grandmothers, uncles, wives and children in their little communities. It would be killing the mother, killing the land, it would signify creating a cataclysm of symbols, passing over a Rubicund of no return. The government will have to put up with them and their fragile wooden rifles, their short stature, their almond-shaped Mayan eyes, their millenary color.

The minors, the "monolinguals," the little Indians have rebelled: David against a disarmed technocratic Goliath with powerful armaments. Their previously anonymous blood is worth more now that it is before the cameras of the world-wide mass media; every rivulet of blood will be captured by those crushing, devouring news machines. It used to be things happened and nobody knew. The blood of that uncomfortable race that stained the dreams of the whites and weighted down their plans to become a replica, a simulacrum of the United States burst out of a silent outrage. These "dwarves" had the luxury of liberating safe and sound a general and former governor of the state who used to endlessly trample upon them, they had they magnanimity to pardon the life of that man who never pardoned theirs. Now, in a new context of typical provincial, ethnic and nationalist wars of autonomy, their cry is all the fashion, not just among the nostalgic losers of the Latin American left. The Indians of Chiapas recreate myths. Their young legend is in the streets in the form of little figures of armed masked men made of fabric and straw, sold by little Indian girls "three for five pesos."

That phrase by Régine Pernoud comes to mind now from her *Vie et mort de Jeanne d'Arc:* "Le plus étonnant portrait de notre histoire: celui d'une fillete qui n'avait pas vingt ans et ne savait a ni b, mais qui a ressuscité un royaume et désigné son roi." ("The most astounding portrait of our history: a girl not yet twenty who couldn't tell a from b, but revived a realm and named its king.")

Christ, Spartacus, St. Francis of Assisi, Joan of Arc, Bolívar, Emiliano Zapata, Lenin, Mao Zedong, Che Guevara, Fidel Castro, Camilo Torres: each country, each region, each continent, desires its heroes and calls out to them.

Saturday, December 31

RIGHT AT DAWN we leave in a Ford pick-up, heading to Guadalupe Tepeyac, where Zapatista troops will celebrate the first anniversary of the rebellion. Omar drives in the foggy dawn light and suddenly the moon appears in all its splendor. Accompanying us once again is Oswaldo Jiménez from the United States, a resident of Alexandria, Virginia. It's cold and the highway is empty because we're the first out and don't want to get in line at the military checkpoint. Beyond Comitán, with the light of day, the guard post finally appears and there we wait almost an hour. Colonel Lara is less tense now and lets us through without much problem. A supposed détente exists and nothing stops us from spending New Year's with the Zapatistas at their famous lair.

After Las Margaritas we delve into beautiful places governed by the law of the "faceless." Yellow-green mountains, idyllic hillsides, the sun on the last day of the year which we will celebrate on the mountain, far from idiotic urban consumerism. We three travelers are all in good spirits, the highway is dry and there are no tree trunks barring the way. The Zapatista Republic in the Lacandon jungle is an ideal Isle of Barataria, with its Quixotes and Sancho

Panzas. As long as this strange animal of man continues to exist on earth, there will be those who rebel and search for an ideal homeland, there will never be a lack of Utopians, rebels, or even those like the crazy station manager in Conrad's *Heart of Darkness*. Everyone wants from time to time to flee civilization for a paradise with neither impositions nor laws, without newspapers or television or huge lighted billboards, whether Robinson Crusoe's famous island or a desert isle filled with bubbling romantic crystalline brooks where one can experience a complete love with a mythical Eve far from the degradations and hate of man, undoubtedly the most terrible beast on the planet.

Far from what one would think, it's only about three hours from the checkpoint to the bastion of Guadalupe Tepeyac, not at all a place in some jungle with crocodiles and jaguars, giant serpents, terrible canyons and savage Indians, as many naïve tourists and journalists think. Not only is San Cristóbal an excellent touristic city with every kind of service, but all along the highway we come across stores with electricity and light filled with sodas, ice cream, fruits and sweets for the tastes of the traveler. Jiménez was sent because the editors are frothing in anticipation of an imminent new massacre. Like the Californian Dan, Oswaldo has been in Haiti and Africa and seen true poverty. Here over the last few days they have had to convince themselves this is something more than a first-class tourist package or a comfortable risk-free safari, that it's a real war to cover.

We continue on calmly and at the first Zapatista checkpoint we find ourselves in the village of El Rosario, where we encounter the rebel bureaucracy. They force us to stop there almost four hours, they take our identification, ask our names, look at us out of the corner of their eyes, they go off to a little house where they communicate by radio and then come back. Those boys here try to act like bureaucrats and detain us even longer than the army. This is politics, this is power: the power to fuck around with you, to take their time and hold consultations, making themselves feel important, to hold the victim beneath the sun and make them beg. Kafka's *The Castle* in guerrilla territory. The wait is terribly boring and I sprawl on the grass next to the genial cameraman Carillo, one of the few agreeable characters I have met here among the journalistic fauna. Later I look at a teeming ant hill and think, Do ants have roadblocks?

In a hammock on a little hillside behind a barbed-wire fence, a Zapatista snoozes with his hat covering his face: the only thing missing is the cactus. Incredibly here comes the famous G., a young woman with beautiful legs and long hair; she heads to the roadblock and they immediately let her by. The jeep carrying her and two other journalists, including a Mexican photographer, speeds past, spraying us with dust. The Mexican journalist happily smiles and no doubt they joke about us stuck here by the work and grace of the Zapatista bureaucrats. The line gets longer with all the regular correspondents, the same international agencies, the identical newspapers, the inevitable faces. Santa G. has passed the roadblock. Already a few of the addicts at the Casa Vieja are in love with her: she's a simple girl who never uses make-up, without exaggerated fear, with the gaze of the ideal faithful beloved. Some of those who envy her have made up love stories about her and the Subcomandante, but there's no proof. I'm on her side, let the envious be left with their words and if it's true that she's the Subcomandante's girlfriend, all the better. No woman today would begrudge her because they all go along with the myth.

Later another journalist I know arrives and he doesn't even wait five minutes. He gets through rapidly and also receives a safe-conduct pass. The chiefs of the Zapatista Isle of Barataria will let other journalists stay another four hours beneath the sun and at that point one starts to imagine just about anything. Nobody protests; it's a slap in the face, but that's normal. On the Isle they follow the arbitrary nature of the official system they are trying to undermine. The chief gives orders from his throne there above on the distant mountain, where just like in the ranchera song "a horseman goes riding." Ten international press cars are in the middle of the highway beneath the beating sun, paying their penance at the whim of the man in charge. Maybe Marcos has the same negative opinion as I do about journalism. At my Isle of Barataria I'd make them wait in the midday sun, too.

After the comings and goings and skirmishes we manage to be let by, but the pleasure doesn't last long. We haven't gone ten minutes before another roadblock stops us after we've passed to the head of the convoy. Again the torture of waiting. Under a zinc-roofed guard post men play cards. On a little table is a book by a friend of mine from Madrid, Luis Méndez Asensio, which relates a trip to Guadalupe after the first battles, but in difficult rainy conditions when real shooting was going on. I have time to look at the map in the book and point out places we're passing through now. They let us by, and after another half-hour, we see the bastion. A cloth banner states "San Pedro Michoacán, Rebel State of Chiapas, Guadalupe Tepeyac," and you can see troop movement, people coming and going, peasants with their bandanas who are arriving to attend tonight's festival. Also located there is the comfortable Ernesto Che Guevara Hospital, refurbished by the Red Cross.

We park and there are the two journalists who came with the ethereal G. They haven't gotten anything done and have been sitting around for hours. A nice spot, a few houses with smoke wafting from them. A man asks me for a cigarette and I give him a couple Colombian Pielrojas I happen to have. Later we head to a café where they sell coffee brewed over a wood fire, fresh chicken soup, beans and rice that taste like heaven. At that place weeks earlier sat waiting Alfredo Molano, one of the most talented and active essayists and writers from my country who has actually gone into the Amazon jungle and penetrated into lands dominated by drug dealers and ferocious guerrillas. He came from Colombia to interview the Subcomandante, but for murky bureaucratic reasons the meeting wasn't granted. Not even his excellent books like *Inner Jungle, Following the court* and other works key to understanding this fiendish country could move the caudillo's heart. "Have him speak with my Moisés and Tacho. He still has some sweating to do before he sees me," Marcos must have said while my friend Molano sipped his coffee in the same place I am now, fashionably awaiting the big show tonight. I wander around deep in thought about memories of childhood trips to villages near the Magdalena River in search of distant relatives.

A family trip to the mountain village of Victoria comes to mind, on one of those buses with observation seats we used to call "Berlinas," down highways spread out between clouds of dust and the nearby torrid vegetation of Ecuador. We're still in the northern hemisphere here in Chiapas, so everything is gentler. I remember on that trip relatives who received us with pleasure and eating lunch outdoors in the sunshine. That night rain fell on the tile roofs and farther off, in the canyons, resounded the rising river thundering down the mountains over a bed of stones. Those lands are where my father's family came from and where he grew up, but that was my first time there. Indelible are the Christmas fireworks, a snake run over in the middle of the street, the robust men of that era, some still standing like hundred-year-old oaks.

We the grandchildren of that enterprising people who spoke with the animals and the trees have bartered everything for the city and consumerism, credit cards, uproar. One must come to a place like this to understand this century's terrible mistake which has led us to the ethics of progress, success and profit. Those old grandparents were concerned with the movement of the winds, the sounds of the night, the aroma of strange plants, the arrival of hummingbirds and migratory flocks, they rested beside lakes and were lulled by the sound of waterfalls in the rural night, but now those sites have already been devoured by progress. Not long ago on a trip back to the city of my birth, I went with a few friends to a beautiful restaurant in a house that used to belong to some neighbors of my family, and I was telling them that the forest of my childhood was the development and avenue they saw out the window of that old house. Everything had disappeared: the enchanted forest of my childhood was a stupid urbanized pile of cement.

Now as I walk through this village, those images come back that through the distance seem unreal. And the recent presence of Molano at this same table has led me to the first voyage I took as an adolescent to Caquetá, sent by my uncle Saul one night on a trip by motorized canoe down a river amidst the whirlpools to the depths of the plains, to the lands of colonizers and guerrillas from where ferocious rivers like the Guayas come. There returns the memory of cattle crossing from one bank to the other, swimming beneath the sun of the plains, lands no doubt more exaggerated in their splendor than those here which are called jungle, although they really aren't. I was fifteen and my uncle, the former guerrilla, sent me to the jungles of Caquetá to "learn to be a man" after criticizing that fact that Álvaro, his brother, was turning me into a little gentleman. It was an unforgettable adventure. On the bus trip to Neiva one hot night, I ended up kissing a girl whose face I never even saw who got off at some lost village. After we passed through Neiva and Florencia we had to wait while they cleared the highway of a landslide. From there to Pueblo Rico, along the expanses of the Lara, I began to experience that other rebel Colombia. After hours going up the river in a motorized canoe, they dropped me off some place and that night I walked among the thickets toward a light I saw in the distance. Those mountains were dominated by the guerrillas and there were often ambushes and killings. The war in Colombia is implacable: the guerillas shoot, ambush, kidnap, kill; the army levels villages, drops bombs, tortures. My uncle, an important player in the Mid-Magdalena, the youngest brother on my father's side, later had a heart attack on a bus and died, but his acts weren't forgotten. After that sole voyage over the plains and through the jungle, I learned not to get lost in any jungle, even the concrete one.

I run across H.B., a blond Mexican writer who looks like Buffalo Bill; he has been here for months since the beginning of the conflict and his search in this region seems profound and contrasts with the silent indifference of most others from our generation. H.B. is a poet and poets, whether they're bad or not, are on the other side, closer to the stones of the rivers and the forgotten hummingbirds than the insensible highway of "progress." Meeting him here does me good. We're having an intense conversation when all of a sudden the masked ones arrive and order us brusquely to get ready to leave. We're going by caravan to Aguascalientes, a few kilometers away, where the ceremonies and big Zapatista parades are taking place. Walking over the grounds in the darkness I exchange a few words with G., the Virgin of Guadalupe from the Casa Vieja, and it's true, she has something special about her that distinguishes her from the other members of the dreamers' club. OK. Good that the Zapatistas let her go through first. She isn't a girl from the "First World" like the other women journalists try to be, with their Ray Ban sunglasses and laptop computers, like caricatures of Sigourney Weaver in "The Year of Living Dangerously," which takes place in Jakarta during a bloody transitional period in Indonesia. G., like H.B., has been here since the outset and like him is looking for something more than simple stories or pictures of Indians. Maybe she's looking for herself. Chance, some subtle incident in her country, has stuck her here in this useless confusion. No doubt she's not the same person who came here a year ago. In the darkness, when I ask her about all these months of coming and going from one village to another far from the damn city, she says to me something like "everything has changed" and she is already "somebody else."

What is it we're searching for? At times in our lives we wish that something outside us, something subtle, would take charge of changing us and so free us from useless routine, from immobility. Why not let Tibet, Katmandu, the Amazon or Ciudad Real change us a little before it's all over? This short cut to Aguascalientes is sort of murky. In a tent the rebels rest in hammocks, arriving from all sides like fireflies with their flashlights. The ground has been cleared for the dances and parades. An enormous Mexican flag hangs over the podium. Hundreds of women and children sit and wait for things to begin. They make coffee and tacos and quesadillas over smoky wood fires. Despite everything it's incredible: in such a submissive country these people have had the courage to create a Quixotean island. The weakest, the most humiliated, have set an example for the country. They are defeated, no doubt, but they shine the light on the ulcer of Mexican apartheid. The clean face of anonymity is over and, really, we should be happy Mexico hasn't entered the First World of the technocrats, the First World that the presidents of the continent's operatic farces invoke like Cerberus tied up before the inaccessible threshold of the great banquet. What is this First World? Is it the infraworld? H.B. offers me a piece of *chicharrón*, fried pigskin, some Zapatistas at a bonfire on the outskirts of Aguascalientes just gave him. He can't eat it. A vegetarian, he doesn't know what to do with the slab; to throw it away would be a crime, a slight to the hosts. I accept it and eat it for him. I take communion with *chicharrón*.

Things get going around midnight, when we're all tired out from the trip and the Kafkaesque wait. Suddenly appear militia members from all sides and on the mountain in the background are seen columns of soldiers with their flashlights titillating in the thickets. People from the village read from a few displays decorated with photos of Che Guevara and Marcos about the history of the Zapatista movement, while the musicians on the stage tune their instruments. The closer it gets to midnight, the more impatient become the journalists after a day and a trip that began before dawn.

Will Marcos come? It's the question everyone asks and more than a few are only here out of some hope of seeing him, filming him, photographing him exactly one year after the beginning of the adventure. All the big press agencies, newspapers and television networks are here, called together by some 400 masked soldiers to the ceremonial place of Aguascalientes. Fifteen-year-old kids talk among themselves in very neat lines, with their little flashlights and worn-out boots, some with red handkerchiefs and other ski masks, but all with the fixed gaze that makes it difficult to distinguish one from the other. Suddenly Amado Avendaño arrives, accompanied by his daughter, who has indigenous features and is dressed in red jeans and a poncho. People break into applause as Moisés greets the "governor of the state of Chiapas" who smiling, with a patch over one eye, consequence of a recent attack on his life, greets the people and begins a speech with all the rhetorical flourish of the old left, including imprecations against the Spanish conquistadors. There are a few musical homages and Captain Maribel salutes her *compañero* Felipe, one of the many who fell in those ten horrible days that shook Mexico. There is a moving moment when the chorus sings a sad melody about the "guerillas who have fallen but still flower," a renting refrain in the middle of the night.

Later they play *marimba* and *batería* to an electric piano and the masked soldiers begin dancing with the teenage Indian girls, clad for the New Year's fiesta in their best dresses of intense phosphorescent blues and reds, adorned with green or purple organdies. Some wear tennis shoes, others plastic shoes. They dance and dance, providing the photographers many opportunities for a perfect shot: little masked men holding in their arms diminutive little girls from some Mayan stele. Then come the parades and the speeches by Comandante Tacho, a severe Indian who is eloquent and clear in his exposition, and then Major Moisés, a short masked man with a huge watch who smokes a pipe, more confusing in his discourse. Midnight arrives and the dance picks up steam. The Californian Dan curses because he has taken three rolls of film of Moisés thinking he was Marcos. Other photographers take pictures of rebels next to a mural of the legendary moustached Emiliano Zapata, the movement's inspiration, a peasant who rebelled against centralized power and died betrayed in Chinameca by General Guajardo.

Is Marcos coming or not? This time everything appears to indicate no; he will leave the press frustrated and they understand when Moisés starts playing a cassette and one hears the fantastic, mythic voice of Marcos coming from some place in the jungle, reading with a hero's perfect diction the "Third Declaration from the Lacandon Jungle," in which he speaks of the governmental party as "the political arm of organized crime and drug trafficking" and describes how "the economic crisis woke Mexicans from the sweet and brutalizing dream of entry into the First World," for which "the federal government has given up custody of the nation."

It is a long proclamation that begins with a quote from a manifesto by Benito Juárez that everyone silently listens to in that strange mountain setting, in the Mexico of the "perfect dictatorship," a cold first day of the year 1995, coming from the voice of the end of the century's romantic young hero. The quote from *Manifesto: standing and resolved like the first day,* proclaimed in Chihuahua by Don Benito Juárez in January of 1865, exactly 130 years ago, is relevant and well chosen:

> 'We have been lucky, it's true; fortune has been against us on many occasions, but the cause of Mexico, which is the cause of right and justice, has not succumbed, has not died and will not die because there still exist valiant Mexicans in whose hearts beats the sacred fire of patriotism, and anywhere in the Republic where they exist clutching arms and the national flag, there as here, will exist the lively and energetic protest of right against power.'

The voice of Marcos is impressive at these altitudes, the messianic voice, the voice of the hidden hero, the prophet, spreading over the mountain. The journalists who crowd around Moisés with their microphones this new year's dawn can barely stand up.

Marcos is undoubtedly a dedicated student, perhaps educated by the Jesuits, for the quote demonstrates he's done his homework well. He reads flawlessly in the tone of the Latin American *caudillo*, but in this case a caudillo that no longer recites Marx or Lenin like his recent Cuban, Colombian, Salvadoran, Nicaraguan and Peruvian predecessors. A few girls who can't take it any longer fall asleep on blankets. Walter, a photographer for a US press agency, has a flashlight on in his backpack and a Zapatista says naively to him he should turn it off before the batteries run out. He looks at the Indian with disdain, taps his nose and says, "I leave it on just because I want to," this amid all the lights and spotlights. He even looks at me like I'm a Martian and then turns away without understanding the diminutive indigenous rebel's astonishment. Here is today's typical journalist, the child of waste, the detestable powerful mercenary who lives off mass media carnage.

The Subcomandante continues to read Juárez's words against Maximiliano, the young usurper monarch placed there by Napoleon III and the local conservatives:

> '...Understand well that this incautious man has accepted the sad mission of being the instrument of a free people's enslavement. His vacillating throne rests not upon the free will of the Nation, but upon the blood and corpses of thousands of Mexicans who have been meaninglessly sacrificed only because they defended their liberty and rights.
>
> Mexicans, having had the misfortune of living under a reign of usurpation,

> do not let yourselves accept the yoke of oppression that weighs upon you. Do not be deluded by the deceptive insinuations of those who belong to the party of accomplished facts, because they are and always have been the party of despotism. The existence of arbitrary power is a permanent violation of right and justice, which neither time nor arms can ever justify, and which it is necessary to destroy for the honor of Mexico and humanity...'

Marcos then reads another personal message and ends with, "Ah, I almost forgot, Happy New Year, just so they can't accuse me of being rude."

The spectators laugh at the unexpected joke. Right then arrive dozens of journalists detained half the night at the roadblocks, and feeling now the bitter sensation of having missed something important. Later Moisés orders the mobilization of the troops who disperse among the nearby gorges as the peasants and special guests wait. Suddenly gunshots ring out, frightening people. M., a journalist who has just arrived, shivers in her cotton shirt not knowing it's just the finale. She has traveled for hours with another friend, just the two women, ready not to miss the party. As pallid and fragile as an archangel, she possesses an extraordinary naturalness, a certain air of intelligence and inner beauty. Maybe this is her first adventure. Her friend's eyes are wide open and other people take cover. Has the massacre begun? Is it an army ambush? A few people try to hide. Others are as pale as corpses.

What's happened is the troops have just shot hundreds of bullets with their fragile .22 caliber rifles, "so it smells like gunpowder and they don't forget this anniversary," says Moisés after the fear subsides and the party picks up with people moving to the music out on the dance floor.

We go with Omar and Oswaldo down a muddy path toward the pick up and run across a photographer who has come all the way to Aguascalientes looking for his new journalist girlfriend. These cinematographic situations are conducive to love.

In Guadalupe Tepeyac I run toward the pick-up of the stern and somewhat snobbish Moisés, who makes things difficult for me and doesn't want to give me the speech. I'm forced to ask G. to intervene on my behalf, and she talks with Major Moisés who scoldingly gives me the copy of the "Third Declaration from the Lacandon Jungle" signed by Marcos. G. is horrified at the way I demand Moisés give me the copy of the document, because I'm not ready to give into the rebel bureaucracy, just as I wouldn't accept similar behavior from the technocratic bureaucracy. I need this document for work reasons, not out of fetishism, I tell her. It was written and edited on a computer in the jungle highlands. This also shows that Marcos is a good student: reading the text I don't find a single grammatical mistake and I feel a kind of professional complicity. It is very well written: fluid, delirious in these political conditions, but acceptable from a literary point of view. We are a continent of proclamations and great literary documents linked to politics. We love pamphlets. Why give up on them?

I kept thinking about my father reading letters by Bolívar, a speech by Don Rafael Uribe Uribe, an address by Benito Juárez, and incendiary texts by modern Colombian Liberals. The voice of the hero Marcos in the mountain silence reminds me of when, on the twenty-fifth anniversary of the death of Jorge Eliécer Gaitán, the Liberal candidate assassinated in Bogotá at a theatre on Seventh Avenue one rainy afternoon, a group of friends from high school and I played a record album with his speeches – on that distant April 9, 1973 — and his voice was powerful, messianic like that of my contemporary tonight. The voice, the speech at the tribunal, is part of our literary tradition and its function corresponds to the idea of politics as art and not an exact science. Now we're governed by economic "scientists" who are frequently wrong and with their speeches have unearthed the ludicrous side of language.

Marcos would be a good theater director, a notable performance artist. Why renounce our tradition of incendiary proclamations and speeches? Nariño, Bolívar, Fray Servando Teresa de Mier, Flora Tristán, Martí, the commune of Galán, Benito Juárez, among other magistrates, must be recuperated for the spectacles of this turn of the millenium. We should dare make a peaceful protest performance, of course, so we can joke about today's Latin American ministers and officials, truly nothings in every sense of the word and a shame to our tradition, because they steal as much as our ancient tribunals but are much less entertaining.

The bottom line is I'm going crazy from fatigue. In a hut they're still making coffee at two in the morning. The only thing left is to lie down in a sleeping bag in a wing at the hospital. I have to sleep between Omar and G. Dozens of attendees lie down in other sectors of the luxurious Hospital Che Guevara. In the cramped sleeping bag I have the worst night of rest I've had in years, perhaps not since at an inn near the Nevado de Ruiz or some rest stop in Europe. Half-asleep I hear them calling G., who gets up and leaves with them. When I wake, instead of her there's some guy next to me.

Sunday, January 1

JANUARY 1 – one year after the Zapatista uprising. The day dawns and the brisk air reminds me of the highlands of my country. Of course we have a delicious unforgettable cup of coffee made from freshly roasted beans over a wood fire that I feel on my body like a felicitous balm. Later we take off down that highway covered with unmasked Zapatistas, going through lands that no doubt will soon be retaken by the army. The trip back is long and tiring because of the highway's bad shape. At Las Margaritas both the federal army and the police from the Interior Ministry copy down all the information from our papers and no doubt we will thus remain for history on the select list of those who went to the Zapatista New Year's celebration in Guadalupe Tepeyac-San Pedro Michoacán-Aguascalientes.

In the afternoon I diligently write articles on the computer about the rebels' anniversary fiesta. They're long texts, one about the "color," as they say in journalistic jargon and another "factual." From where I'm writing at the restaurant of the Hotel Bonampak one can see a strange pinkish mansion, enormous and half-abandoned sitting amidst the empty lots. It looks like it's from the '30s or '40s, perhaps it's an old hacienda, a cloistered school, a rooming house from the past. I already feel nostalgic about the end of this passage through San Cristóbal and the Zapatista highways. In the distance are the city, peaks, mountains. We work hard, but we also feel a lot. This has been more than work. Our eyes have a different gaze, not concerned with news, because here there is no big news: just a daily example of the microscopic history of some corner of Latin America.

I love the way the year begins — sleepless, vigilant, buzzed on a couple beers this first day of January, but with the pen alive, that marvelous pen that has always nourished us. The pink mansion leads me immediately to wild imaginings of ghosts, children roving through corridors, old women weaving, young consorts full of illusions, music, sound, life. In the afternoon light the building rests there like a poem not yet written with burdens from the past I perceive.

Down the avenue pass military vehicles with soldiers, even some tanks, and from a strange vehicle full of antennas emitting signals jump out a few military officers who go sit at a table beside the road. They pass pleasant tranquil hours, they request expensive wines, they make toasts, they recall youthful adventures and missions in other states, they get drunk together like old buddies: for decades the Mexican military has not taken offensive military actions of any kind, although the opposition still insistents upon bringing up the shots fired at the Plaza de Tlatelolco in 1968. Chiapas has put the army on guard and given them a reason for being.

For saying something ironic about the supposed bravery of his country's soldiers, the writer Juan Rulfo experienced the fury of Mexican *presidencialismo* in that distant year of 1981. All he said was the only "cannon balls" the military has ever known are made of money, and the high command, which had just paid homage to him a few weeks earlier at the Palace of Fine Arts, scolded his daring with a sinister display of power. Now who remembers the name of the president at the time? Rulfo lived thereafter in a kind of limbo: the great Rulfo, author of *Pedro Páramo* and *El llano en llamas,* an extraordinary photographer who left thousands of negatives, a true living legend in his country whom all Latin America recalls with veneration.

Too many writers everywhere in the world, and of course on this continent, are beings too worried about their image, their "career." They don't sleep from scheming about intrigues against potential rivals, they get ulcers when they don't receive an invitation to attend a function at the palace and they suffer when they aren't in fashion.

Rulfo, on the contrary, was absorbed in his books and memories, lost in his modest office at the National Indigenist Institute located in the south of Mexico City, sipping a cup of coffee served him by his faithful secretary of years or passing entire afternoons chatting in the bookstores El Ágora and El Juglar with young people and old friends. He clearly perceived with certainty that everything is in vain, but felt as well the intensity of his passage on this earth. He was the kind of writer who doesn't write because it's a "career" or to complete something for his editor: he wrote what he had to write and success, glory didn't turn him into a prima donna. He comes from the same race as Samuel Beckett, Émile Cioran, Enrique Molina, Elias Canetti among contemporary wise men who, connected as they were with death and its mysteries, saw farther than others. The scandal prompted by Rulfo's inoffensive joke about the military had repercussions that must have made bitter the last pieces of his life. Many times I went to the cafeteria at El Agora when Rulfo was there, where he spent hours alone with a cup of coffee and his halo of authenticity. Concerning the work of Rulfo and his country, the nettlesome Mexican writer Federico Campbell has recently written in his book *The Invention of Power* that Mexico, "where legality is only invoked as an alibi," is best represented by the fictional town of Comala and its "reign of impunity." Like the presidents of Mexican history, "Pedro Páramo answers to no one; and so, little by little, over the years since its publication in 1955, the novel *Pedro Páramo* has become the great metaphor of Mexican power, the quintessence of the *cacique* and presidential absolutism, the methods of the authoritarian presidency, the style of Mexican power."

The great drama of intellectuals here as in all of Latin America is that often any criticism of the system is considered "betraying the nation" if done by a native, or a "campaign of insults" if the opinion of a foreigner. A lot of people still hate the English writers Malcolm Lowry, D.H. Lawrence and Graham Greene because they at one time described the arbitrary nature of things seen in the heartland of Mexico and the arbitrary nature that reigns over the entire continent. The drama of nationalism is in vogue throughout the world, which at times unites enemies in placing before the outlander's gaze a veil hiding the truth. The torturer and the tortured unite to defend national "prestige" and "greatness."

In an essay on Mexican art, Octavio Paz said in this respect that the "function of nationalism is to cover a wound, hide what is lacking, disguise a reality that shames us." And here right beside me, amidst wine and big platters plays out the party of those soldiers in the war that for almost a year hasn't felt the clamor of bullets. Those subject to Rulfo's irony are happy and calm this first day of the year. Suddenly the well-known former rector of the National University, Pablo González Casanova, comes into the restaurant in his muddy boots and it seems curious to me that the old independent humanist, almost seventy, one of that kind which almost no longer exists and is stigmatized for being naïve or full of illusions by the rational adepts of the market place, crosses paths with the soldiers and in this micro-world of causalities and signs eats lunch along with a young disciple, his daughter and his grandson. Life in this incessant trajectory brings that man from another epoch here, full of enthusiasm because finally after so many books written and speeches given his country appears to be on the move. But is it really moving? Is all this just a game of masks?

Tonight, my last evening in these lands, I overcome fatigue and go to the farthest reaches of the city. I climb the peak of San Cristóbal and from there try to discern streets and churches. This desolate first day of the year is cold. The taxi driver climbs the hill with me and explains in detail the streets and buildings I point to. He was born here and tells me about his childhood, the processions, the aunts who used to bring him up to these heights, dinners, distant events.

When I'm in a city more than a couple weeks, something of it remains in me. That's what happened with Tegucigalpa, where I stayed at a Holiday Inn for three weeks almost ten years ago, hallucinating with the screeching black magpies, the plaza stopped in the old modernist decade of the '20s, in the desolate and infernal misery of Camayagüela. It happened to me in Stockholm, Frankfurt, Berlin, Bordeaux, Barcelona, Los Angeles, New York and especially Rome. On this dead day they come back to me like friends.

Cities becomes lovers. I wasn't a tourist in San Cristóbal. It had to be like that this winter, so I could think, and think about myself, so I could recover from the confusion of other recent voyages. Rightfully so this is a Borgesian night, especially this absurd trip on foot into the hills to the heights of the city, although I've hardly slept in the last fifty hours. Later I go to the other peak, Guadalupe, and walk on staircases that hang from the hillsides where I see old streets with their houses of terra cotta tile roofs. The place has a strange abandoned air, the wind violently blows about scraps of paper. Later I ask the taxi driver to drop me off at the Zócalo and from there I keep walking and bidding my farewells.

Monday, January 2

I TAKE ONE last look at the Cathedral and the streets downtown. I eat breakfast in the same place I usually have with my newspapers, magazines or some book. The bustle has returned to the city after the end of the New Year's festivities. The ideological tourists walk around astonished and happy, surrounded by little Indian girls who sell them colored bracelets or dolls of Ramona and Marcos. I walk down the street past the restaurant El Teatro and an old building being restored and hurry for my last visit to the former convent of Santo Domingo.

With just a few hours to go everything seems more intense. In the little plaza of the precious church are hundreds of Indians who have set out their weavings, clothes, rugs, bags, belts and handicrafts that are snatched up by the tourists. Amidst the people run dozens of Indian children playing and speaking Tzotzil and Tojolabal.

I hurry to the church, for I want to scrutinize one last time the Baroque altars and the minutely detailed pulpit, jewels from a time gone by. Are we Baroque?, I'm thinking, drunk this last midday on the pure golden images next to the twisted and magisterial eighteenth century pulpit, considered one of the most notables altars in Latin America, when by some miracle comes out of the darkness Oswaldo Jiménez, the US photographer of Ecuadorian origin. It's incredible, he's the only person I told about this marvelous church, recommending a visit before he left, and now we run into each other here.

The energy of the literati: at the lunch Christmas Eve at El Teatro, I made him a list of Latin American authors I suggested he read in order to recuperate the literary roots of his lost lands, and he has already bought *Ficciones* and a book of poetry by Borges. Now he takes a photo of the souls of wood devoured by red eternal fire that were sculpted centuries ago, fixed beneath a vintage retable. One of the most fascinating concepts of Catholicism, souls enchant me: souls that exist forever and in some temporary way purge our sins with flames in a gaze of resignation, hands clasped in a tone of prayer or desperation.

That's what we are in a certain way, souls. This world is purgatory. Could there be even more purgatory to come? Oswaldo appreciates, too, the beauty of those colorful little figures only a foot high that create an incredible aesthetic impact, placed here beside a Baroque golden wall. I love the squeaking of the dusty old wooden floor, I'm seduced by the semi-dark interior and the radiant sun outside. In March of 1545 a contingent of monks coming from Salamanca arrived and two years later they began constructing the convent and church, finished in 1560. More than four centuries have passed and the rustic façade of pink marble is still intact, atop which still shines the two-headed eagle of the Hapsburgs and the imperial coat-of-arms of Carlos I of Spain.

We decide to eat at a restaurant right out front whose walls are adorned by tapestries woven with Mayan designs. Here comes one of those young U.S. humanitarians, this time a pallid brunette, happy because her father is coming to visit her San Cristóbal adventure. "He's a good guy," she tells me, happy to see the old man who came from who knows where to spend a few moments with her. She is one of the people those in the thrall of the modern technocrats disdainfully call "Sandalistas," heirs of the dreamy St. Francis evoked by Rubén Darío. The meal is delicious and we lift our beers in toast. Time is running short. I say goodbye to Oswaldo.

In a warm and inviting bookstore I find by chance Emir Rodríguez's book about Neruda, *The Unmoving Traveler.* The Chilean poet should have no doubt come to Chiapas and after his visit he would have written odes to the Indians, to the minerals, to the woods and weavings. I'm impressed by the great selection here at Chilam Balam, not far from Santo Domingo at 33 General Utrilla Street, at the corner of Doctor Navarro, an old place with a Spanish patio run by an ill-tempered Frenchman. On the other side of the plaza I find a beautiful piece of folk art: a demon possessing golden horns and a penetrating gaze, its black serpentine body flecked with yellow, blue, green and red, its trembling wings made of golden membrane. It's a one-of-a-kind. I buy this devil to put on my work desk next to my computer. When the afternoon is almost finally over, I walk one last time under the still vibrant sun to Santo Domingo and bid farewell. When I get back to the house to pack my bag, it's already twilight.

Next to a silent military tank parked in front of a restaurant where I quickly ate breakfast so many times, I stop a taxi that takes me to Tuxtla Gutiérrez. The trip down the dangerous highway snaking toward the hot lands is delicious. It's almost night and the moon is huge. The clouds again have turned an unreal blood red and metallic silver. Strange masses, a kind of virtual reality, they would make a most excellent setting for a crepuscular work. You could transfer them to 1896 London and Huysman, Beardsley, Moreau.

What a pleasure to let the wind blow in my face, to feel the wind messing up my hair while the taxi speeds along, devouring the guardrails. There is the hot, modern city: the provincial capital with avenues, traffic congestion, buildings, billboards, corrupt police. One of them stops the car and wants to extort the driver. He asks for our identification, in the end the traditional strategy for eliciting a bribe. I want to get to my hotel, to a big wide bed in a room at the top so I can look out at the lights of progress. I'm impressed by Tuxtla and this broad bustling avenue full of stores and neon signs amidst the cement that still retains the stifling heat despite the night. This is the typical Latin American provincial city which desires to emulate the great urbs: cement buildings, billboards, stop lights, a few trees and parks, bustling crowds moving from one place to another.

I finally arrive to the Camino Real, located at the top of a hill, a somber edifice recently constructed whose contemporary architecture has become the pride of this city. The rate in dollars is quite cheap because of the recent galloping devaluation of the peso, but I still try to get a discount, which at first they won't give me. The lobby is welcoming and I have to admit I love these kinds of hotels, even if I do shout in protest about modernity. But I have always loved the Camino Real, characterized by that modern Mexican architecture that lends them their peculiarity, compared to some of those horrendous hotel chains I've stayed at where in whatever corner of the world you find the same antiseptic environment, with their synthetic carpet and plastic plants. I look down below at the swimming pool all lit up, the fake waterfalls echoing among the trees and reflecting off the orange-colored walls. In the stores abound soaps and luxury skin products next to magazines of every kind coming from every continent. The smell of newness spreads throughout the corridors in this universe that isolates us from the poor who wander down the modern avenues of progress.

I fall into the delicious bed in the comfort of this recently inaugurated superhotel smelling of newness, the most luxurious place in Tuxtla: five stars, grand tourism, blue waterfalls, relaxing music, orange corridors and walls, the greatest building in the city, a kind of inaccessible and ultramodern tower only an hour from colonial San Cristóbal. On the television is CNN and news of the new year, turning the channel is some movie with actress Sharon Stone: the son of the legendary Kirk Douglas penetrates her violently on a king-size bed and the two come sweating and screaming. Stone is on top of him and looks like she wants to kill him. The pope, trembling and sick, delivers a New Year's message: he continues to ask, like his predecessors, punishment for a world where at times the Catholic priests are the most lascivious and perverse people of all. The Mexican government hasn't rested and is doing everything possible not to hang itself any further: on the screen are the faces of ministers dedicated to giving useless confidence to the population, although from all appearances everything is about to crash. Elton John spins around a piano on some clownish stage. Music videos with rock stars follow one after the other: Madonna, Nirvana, U2, Guns-n-Roses, Suzanne Vega. Among the Latinos and Hispanic Americans are Gloria Estefan, Julio Iglesias, the sexy Rosario, Marta Sánchez, Luis Miguel. On another channel is a film from the '40s with the Indio Fernández, cowboys, Indians with sombreros and a moustached mariachi singer who serenades a woman wearing a *rebozo*.

The passage is over and tomorrow I return to Mexico City. I finally bathe with scented soap and slather myself with skin cream. The moustached man wins a kiss from the woman in wide skirts and long braids. The Pope blesses again the multitude at St. Peter's. Masked Zapatistas dance in Aguascalientes with young Mayan women for just a second on a still from a U.S. news show. I recognize a diminutive Indian teenager dressed in an electric blue skirt and tennis shoes dancing with a masked Zapatista, and I think how the photographer must have tried to look for the best angle. The gringa actress is still fucking Michael Douglas. The cowboy kisses the rancher's daughter wearing a shawl and then rides away on his horse. Latin American presidents make optimistic New Year's speeches. Now the actress Stone comes to her lesbian lover at an enormous beautiful mansion where she writes crime novels. A bombardment of advertising: the Marlboro man, the latest car, perfume, shampoo, Trojan condoms. I sleep like a rock after two weeks of fatigue.

Tuesday, January 3

FROM HIGH ABOVE, as the plane slowly cruises toward the metropolis, the view of Mexico City is striking. During all my years living here, I have returned by plane to the capital a hundred times from different places around the country and the world and on this occasion I am struck by the same curiosity as the first time. This is the biggest city on earth: the plane passes minute after minute over a tapestry of lights that not even the prophet Jules Verne could have imagined.

There are dozens and dozens of lesser cases in the world like Mexico City, but because of its complexity, it has become the archetype of the great mistake we have been speaking so much about. The reflection of progress, animated as much by the forces of economic liberalism as communist statism, led to the creation of these cities that are versions of a planetary cancer. All the residents of a country work to nourish these useless monsters full of parasites brought together by the ambition of development, opportunity, and the future. These urban tumors suck the life out of their countries and extend over the countryside in a kind of apocalyptic dance.

In the nineteenth century the Mexican landscape painter José María Velasco depicted the extensive Valley of Anáhuac. From atop one of the nearby peaks, the artist shows us from his time this land of unequaled beauty with its view of volcanoes, crests, hills and lakes whose clarity could still be seen until recently, because the present monstrosity has only emerged over the last thirty years. Foreign visitors who stayed and old Mexicans still remember how in the '50s one could enjoy the impressive late afternoons of a strange pale violet and gold, when the avenues still had trees and people walked in a land made to the measure of man. They recount how until just a couple decades ago they used to swim in rivers or play on great fields, today covered by cement and horrible buildings.

The current city is the kingdom of suffocation: wind doesn't reach the streets, the air is stagnant, the sun heats the asphalt and the temperature rises, noise surpasses acceptable decibel levels for human hearing, every day the car — lord and master — expels ominous polluted air and smashes into dozens of human beings whose deaths barely merit becoming a statistic. Over twenty million human beings remain plastered together here below while planes circle in the air waiting to land at Benito Juárez Airport. They never see the stars, seldom do they have time to stop and look at a tree much less think about the moon.

I know I'm returning to the Inferno and the contrast with San Cristóbal is immediate and terrifying: yesterday I stood before the former convent of Santo Domingo with its rustic façade, in another century that fortunately still survives and now, in the blink of an eye, I'm standing in line to get a taxi, surrounded by luminous billboards, tanned tourists, businessmen about to have a heart attack. Citizens are proud of the city's progress, its model reproduced endlessly throughout the world, devouring even my city,

Manizales. Just a few months ago, I was relating to a few friends how the forest of my childhood, the paradise of games and adventures, had been converted into a horrible urbanization of cement and musty yellow street lights, my crystal hilltops now notched with the machines of civilization and progress. Technocrats destroy old buildings and their grandparents' homes with patios full of primroses and vines in order to make way for new avenues. They're ecstatic when historic fronts fall and bulldozers plow over childhood parks, old neo-classical theaters, flowering trees.

Because of the wealth of its imagination, throughout the twentieth century Mexico nourished minds from throughout the Americas through films of the Golden Epoch, endless popular music, the revolutionary heroes Pancho Villa and Emiliano Zapata, unforgettable writers like José Vasconcelos, Alfonso Reyes, Juan Rulfo, Carlos Fuentes and Octavio Paz, painters such as Diego Rivera, Frida Kahlo, José Clemente Orozco and Rufino Tamayo. Due to its proximity to the United States, it has followed the example of constructing a luminous urb of progress and over the last few years has accelerated the path toward integration with its northern neighbor.

The fate of Mexico is the fate of the rest of the Americas and its destiny has been our own since the epoch of the pyramids through the Baroque centuries to the gestures of Independence, the first signs of progress and the delirium of the twentieth century. This great city is proof of the mistake of the mid-century politicians who bet on the gods of the automobile and the skyscraper. For other countries which have yet achieved this madness, its bloody wound should be a warning at the turn of the millenium that they must conserve human spaces before destroying them with the insanity of highways. It's not strange that this country, generator of imaginary beings and images for the continent, has produced out of its guts the lucid new call of the Indians, of the discardable.

Zapatismo has little to do with those sectarian guerilla movements that flourished during the '60s and '70s with their sinister doctrines whose action was the counterpart of the doctrine of military security, with its terse colonels and nameless torturers. Montoneros, Tupamaros, the Shining Path and other Marxist guerillas have nothing to do with this unique cry from the jungles of Chiapas, itself seemingly useless because the problem is unsolvable, but still valid for the absurd mark it makes. At the beginning, in a dogmatic reaction, the intellectual spokesmen of free enterprise and market economics, who offer precepts that don't hold up at the moment of bankruptcy, immediately condemned those Indian rebels. Weeks later they had to admit sorrowfully that this voice was something else, with another intention and without a goal of taking power. These eyes have seen them from the peaks and canyons of Chiapas: the incredulous technocrats, until recently infallible, can't accept that the monolingual disposables, who still dress as they did in pre-Hispanic times, might have a voice and speak out.

The existence of these diminutive characters and their inadmissible stubbornness is a kind of nightmare for the unfeeling capitalist project. Germán Arciniegas, the Colombian author of the well-known *Biography of the Caribbean,* states in *The Student of the Round Table* (1932) the monk Tomás Ortiz's express opinion about the Indians in demanding their perpetual servitude:

> "The men of the *terra firma* eat human flesh and are worse Sodomites than any previous generation. Justice does not exist among them; they walk about naked; they feel nei-

> ther love nor shame; they are asses, simple-minded, half-witted, insensible; they think nothing of killing themselves or committing murder; they value getting drunk and make wine of different herbs, fruits, roots and grains; thcy also get drunk by smoking and ingesting certain herbs that make them crazy; they are bestial in their vices; they are traitorous, cruel, vengeful people who never forgive, apers of religion, harangues, lying thievery and low, mean-spirited judgments; they are witches, diviners, necromancers; they are as scared as little rabbits, as dirty as pigs; they eat every kind of bug, spider and raw worm they find; they have neither the art nor skill of men; it seems that until about ten years ago they still carried some education and virtue; since then they have turned into brute animals; I would finally say that God never created such a people so mired in vice and bestiality.'

Right now these same thoughts come out of the mouths of local political strongmen, ranchers, white shopkeepers, and government and military officials, upset by the million Indian rebels of Chiapas. On the twentieth of December, I heard the *ladinos* of Simojovel express opinions more or less like those of Ortiz: they spoke of the lack of skills, the stubbornness and the insensateness of those aborigines. At the turn of the millenium there they are with their cancerous presence and the continent still hasn't found an answer to their reality.

At Benito Juárez Airport I see Amado Avendaño's daughter, with her dark-skinned indigenous face and her modern gear: leather jacket, red jeans, scarf and cell phone. And there's another girl walking around, white as can be, all dressed in denim with no make-up and long straight hair, two sides of the same Latin American coin at this end of the century. At the airport in Tuxtla I ran into the director of the Mexican edition of the Madrid newspaper *El País,* Fernando Orgambides, with whom I engaged in a wonderful polemic a few months ago during a round-table at the National Museum, where I told him, to the astonishment of those in attendance, that his optimistic view of Mexico's near future was a story out of Walt Disney. That day I left the table and hastily departed after setting up one those happenings I like to create from time to time just to challenge mediocre bureaucrats. I don't have anything in particular against Walt Disney and even owe many happy childhood moments to his characters, but at times I think the ideology of technocrats has remained in the imaginary world of rich Uncle McDuck and they direct their countries like comic strips, except their mistakes have cruel consequences for millions of citizens. Months later we meet in a country now under a cloud, with the rich Uncle McDucks beaten up.

I like the way Spaniards and Colombians have the spontaneous ability to argue and say what they think without it turning into a big drama. In Mexico, after decades of domination by one sole political party, people have been more careful and conferences in general have a courteous limit where nothing much is risked. With more and more frequency, for a Mexican politician or intellectual to participate on a round table organized by a rival clan can signify literary or political death and from there comes the reasonable fear of compromising oneself, because a single phrase can be mortal. Only an admirable type like Mario Vargas Llosa could stand up against an important group of Mexico's thinkers who had exonerated the country from also belonging to the totalitarian and *caudillista* Latin American tradition. His definition of the "perfect dictatorship" has become a historical phrase and is reproduced in graffiti on streets throughout the country.

This is why Marcos and the Zapatistas are important: they are the first members of their generation to lower the veils to the world and say what they think, to dare say they assume custodianship of the flag and the national anthem because the government no longer deserves this honor, to raise their voice against the wicked petty despot and the obtuse *Criollo* technocrat. At first a good part of the country's intellectuals were angered by the appearance of these killjoy Indians, but as the years pass they will realize the importance of their defeated gesture. They have cut the umbilical cord with the State party, the all-powerful and paternal "philanthropic ogre" of which Octavio Paz spoke. Marcos and the Zapatistas passed the Rubicund when they fired the first shots against the immovable, technocratic tyrant that, like everywhere on the continent, has no moral authority to speak of "civil society" or "rule of law" when it violates them on a daily basis. The astonishment of that symbolic gesture continues here, even in its obvious weakness and ineluctable failure.

The rhetoric of technocrats about "democracy" and "law" is one of the most horrible farces of Latin American history: only the most cynical and stupid can believe in a democracy conducted through the televised manipulation of the masses, where on the screens the clean-cut faces of the presidency, a very tolerant lot, only hide their lies about dirty business, enterprises privatized in the name of their friends or other fronts, illegal insider trading and handing over their country to a few clans. The entire Latin American middle-class has been hypnotized by the "power of your signature" on their credit cards and elections are nothing more than a farce where the same people as ever are ratified. In the fictitious world of advertising the technocrats are indeed most skillful: Latin Americans are today as enslaved as they were during the times of Porfirio Diáz and the company stores, as during the era of *Mamita Yunai* and the rubber workers of Casa Arana, the epoch of Ricardo Güiraldes, Rómulo Gallegos and José María Arguedas.

At that round-table everybody said Mexico was doing fine, there would be no economic crisis and capital would continue flowing into the country despite what was happening in Chiapas, and even before I put on my show (in the opinion of that official audience convoked by the newspaper *El Día)* I had looked like some kind of crazy, eccentric being who crashed the party. Now, with questions still unresolved about the Mexican technocratic project and the corrupted dream of joining the "First World," I understand my opinions that day weren't simply those of some anachronistic person skeptical of the arrival of the happy, fetterless world of free enterprise and market economics.

Now we return to the great capital and find ourselves submerged in another crisis caused by the fall of ministers, capital flight, rising interest rates, further devaluations of the peso, bankrupt businesses and so many ruined people who believed in the power of credit cards and bank loans. I went to Chiapas two weeks ago with the country on a honeymoon, ready to follow the path of the First World, and I return to another scene typical of Latin America: the end of the euphoric magicians of technocracy, the mask of reality lifted, savings absconded in capital flight and people once again tricked and crestfallen.

Every Latin American generation since the last century has lived through this recurring chapter: foreign debt, bankruptcy, loss of sovereignty, poverty, never-ending histories like the revolutionary hero, the bishop, the general and the president, the viceroy, the dictator or the cabinet member who flees with a suitcase full of dollars. But there's something that startles me and that's the growing cowardice of intellectuals and "clerks," those who have been bought off with the possibility of enjoying a miserable little sinecure in this fiesta of modernity. Writers have become little employees of publishing houses, meek columnists for the newspapers which dominate every country, beautiful jeweled little pets with tamed words, slavering with ambition so they'll be accepted by politicians, bureaucrats, and editors. They have lost the rebellion of the great pamphleteers of our continent who would rather have lived in obscurity than cower before the powerful.

I think my generation, that of post-'68, composed of those born in the '50s and '60s, has become indifferent to misery and is now the accomplice of its agents. They have a full stomach and so think it's obsolete, anachronistic, naïve to raise their voice against the great farce which neo-liberals and economists have made out of the continent of Simón Bolívar. The world has no order, but the writer, the prophet, the philosopher must become the uncomfortable critic and pricking conscience of his time, not today's worn out little employee with his sparse words, his "career" molded according to the interests and taste of cultural functionaries, politicians, and the great vampire publishing houses.

I love thinking about the recent grandees of this *novo hispano* continent, like that madman Bolívar, a hero and excellent writer who died impoverished and humiliated by those he helped liberate from the Spanish yoke, whose texts *A Response by an Equatorial American to a Gentleman of this Island,* better known as *Letter from Jamaica,* and *My Delirium about the Chimborazo* still have a seductive quality. At the end of his life, students and opponents of militarism considered him a dictator and his drunken lieutenants trampled upon his glory and laurels. Skeletal and sick, he knew that nobody listened any longer to his incendiary oratorical language. A grand visionary, he predicted the future of each new nation, diagnosing their vices and ineluctable tendencies.

The end of the heroic Bolívar is that of all Latin American rebels who achieve power and who like Fidel Castro, the Sandinistas and many others, end up involved in ignominy, intolerance, dirty business, unjust firing squads, and nepotism, which might make us to wish that rebels never achieved power. The Latin American poet, writer or novelist, out of tradition a prophet as were José Martí, Jorge Isaacs, Leopoldo Lugones, and Rómulo Gallegos, is an institution whose future existence seems guaranteed as long as the distance between the wealthy elite and the increasing number of poor becomes more cancerous and terrible. The prophet will have to cry out against the false continental democracy made of advertising, public relations, intrigue, corruption and intolerance.

I take pride and fortune in never having voted, of having never stained my finger with the ink of this farce and so not be the useful idiot of the infamous political caste of my own country and the whole continent: the vote of the writer must be the poem, the novel, the pamphlet, the sniper's trigger finger in face of the hypocritical tyranny of the economists and all their acolytes. Their hypnotic capability has convinced many, including their victims, that the poor, the broken, the Indians, the low-lifes are disposable beings whose fate doesn't matter. Its project is one of a continent divided between a wealthy elite living in Miami or Houston or bunkers in the capitals and on the other side today's pariahs, more distanced than ever from education and nourishment, condemned to infamous slums and paid pennies in order to satisfy the pressure for "low overhead," "cost/benefit analysis," "competitiveness." A continent of physical laborers that technocrats consider irrational soulless beings unable to reason (as occurred during the Colonial era with the indigenous people and the black slaves), their only diversion television and its virtual reality perfumed with impeccable blond models, goddesses from the unreachable heights of consumerism. The lost Latin American cities like Nezahualcóyotl in Mexico City and Ciudad Bolívar in Bogotá and the wretched shacks of the slums of Caracas and Rio de Janeiro, not to mention Lima, Santiago and Panamá among other capitals, indeed exist but seem to have disappeared by the work and grace of a technocratic hypnotism pledged to believe that the "First World" of a few hundred impresarios, the First World of selfish elites, is the reality of 400 million Spanish-speaking hominoids at the turn of this millenium in the lands of the New World.

The ideology of neoliberalism has managed to convince many that numbers are everything and the pride of a nation resides in its technocrats being praised by Wall Street for the glorious task of reducing the salaries of its fellow citizens to nothing, showing off the miserable skeletal wages like some kind of trophy from an African safari. Today anything that touches on this theme is considered anachronistic, out of touch with history, romantic, naïve, anti-patriotic, resentful, terroristic words spoken by an enemy of progress or a saboteur of development and democracy or a murdering communist.

Modern man is told he must be impassive to the killings of disposable beggars in Río or Bogotá, the hunger of Indians and peasants in Mexico, the fate of the impoverished in Caracas or the little black-haired kids in Buenos Aires or the hidden poor of Santiago de Chile who aren't allowed into the downtown of the capital so as not to mar the statistics of the gleaming storefronts. The model countries of Latin America are those that show "growth," but growth for what reason and for whom? Chile and Argentina win medals of honor for their numbers while the genocidal dictator Augusto Pinochet and his version of military cowboys pass impudently through the world. In every country a handful of businesses monopolizes everything and takes over the means of communication, making invisible any newspaper or publishing house that dissents from the technocracy, which is no doubt quite useful in matters of administration and accounting, but unworthy of providing a country with imagination. Justice is applied in a selective manner according to the orders of the vampiristic, parasitical capitalists. The minority of privileged students accepted at private universities often turn their backs on the fellow members of their generation from the hinterlands, who are for them soulless, irrational beings: simple failures.

This is the Royal City I've returned to after the trip to San Cristóbal de las Casas, where another episode of regional history is written, fortunately more with words than bullets. Chiapas has demonstrated the power of the word and literature, just as Octavio Paz himself confirmed in recognizing the media skills of the postmodern guerilla Marcos. Language and writing have yet to die. Their power is a key weapon in making visible the totalitarianism of capital and solidifying the achievements obtained in the struggle against intolerance by the humanitarian prophets still left on this planet: the dreaming heirs of St. Francis, of the hermit, of the crazy monk, of Robin Hood. Words into the wind. Useful words? In they air they screech, burn, send electric shocks against the forces of the money god and the automobile god, deities that take pride in the end of nature and the planet.

A cruel and unpitying elite of new Attilas with an ethics of accumulation desires to become the paradigm of our contemporary world. When the model cracks and man is forced to renounce consumerism and return to the simplicity of past epochs, respecting the beggar's cup and the torn shirt, celebrating the sunrise and the song of birds by the river, there amidst the aromas of the flora those people will think a great mistake our epoch and the mythical "First World" our representatives so desire: cancerous cement cities, green spaces destroyed day after day because of an insensible materialism where people were valued by what they bought and not by what they were. Nineveh fell, Egypt fell, Greece fell, Rome fell, Byzantium fell, Spain fell, France fell, England fell, the Soviet Union fell, and one day will fall the kingdom of consumption.